2019

The author is a friend who changed our [lives].

Life. May you find morsel from experience and wisdom.

Live lovingly always.

It is all that matters.

:)

PRAISE FOR
EXCEPTIONAL EVERY DAY

"Jason's chapter on balancing work and passion would single-handedly justify the book. *Exceptional Every Day* is a must-read if you want to do what you love and get paid for it."

—DEREK DEPREY, author of *SHIFT: Move from Frustrated to Fulfilled*; Director of People & Service, Wisconsin Athletic Club

"Jason has written a book that is a must-read for anyone striving for personal excellence. Leveraging experiences and anecdotes from his past, he reveals specific concepts, principles, and techniques that can help you unlock the hidden potential that resides within you. Read this book, and accelerate your journey to a more successful and happier life!"

—MIKE ETTORE, Founder, Fidelis Leadership Group, LLC

"The fame of being a TV star rocked my world and thrust me into a tailspin of seeking external validation. Through his book *Exceptional Every Day*, Dr. Valadão helped me face myself in the mirror, dig deep, and love myself from within. If you find yourself lost in the chaos of modern life, this is a book that will help you find the clarity that we all need."

—COMMANDER ANDREW BALDWIN, M.D., United States Navy, star of *The Bachelor*

"This bestseller is a must in your journey! Dr. Jason Valadão's empowering process of leading you to a better life will bring results that you have been seeking in this world of confusion and uncertainty. From the first day I met Dr. Valadão, I've been inspired and transformed by his wisdom, knowledge, and desire to serve. Thank you, Dr. Valadão, for your service and the value you bring to my life."

—CARLA ANDREWS, President and Chief Inspirational Officer, Signature Living, Inc.

"An amazing book that uses personal stories to generate insight and reflection. You will use The Process on your journey to becoming the best 'you' that you can be."

—CAPTAIN MARIA A. YOUNG, Commanding Officer, United States Navy, Naval Hospital, Guam

"A remarkable book from someone who lives The Process and communicates its value with great examples—especially his own journey."

—ALAN K. DAVID, M.D., Professor and Chair, Department of Family and Community Medicine, Medical College of Wisconsin

"Masterful description of life. It's not where you start, but where you finish!"

—REV. DEAN M. VIESELMEYER, Ph.D., Professor and Advisor, Master of Arts/Science in Coaching and Athletic Administration, Concordia University, Irvine

"An inspirational journey of a young man and the lessons he learned along the way."

—DIAN VIESELMEYER, former Dean of Student Success and Director of Academic Advising, Concordia University, Irvine

"Jason best articulates how passion combined with a focus on The Process leads to exceptional success. His framework helped take me from walk-on to 1000-yard rusher in the Pac-12 Conference."

—PATRICK LAIRD, student-athlete and NFL hopeful, University of California, Berkeley

"An informed and inspiring read by one of my most respected and successful young Naval Officers. Jason's passion and drive for life come alive as he pulls you into his journey and encourages you to align your priorities each and every day!"

—KARL THOMAS, Rear Admiral, United States Navy

"The Process provides readers at any stage in life with the realistic framework needed to not only take control of their priorities but also maintain them and enjoy a life that is truly fulfilling, one exceptional day after another."

—BETTINA SAUTER, D.O., Commander, United States Navy

"*Exceptional Every Day* is a touching, highly self-reflecting adventure with much to say about reestablishing what really matters in our lives. Jason Valadão takes us through The Process that is our 'lives' in a way that no one else has. This is an inspiration for everyone looking to align their various passions with purpose."

—PAUL MARTINELLI, international speaker and mentor

"This book made me want to flag pages, write in the margins, and highlight constantly. Within the first few pages, I redefined my Why, something that has been an important part of my Process for more than twenty years. Having a large network marketing organization and being an admiral's wife have taught me that you have to learn and grow constantly. Jason's teaching on The Process is a must for anyone wanting to change their lives for the better. Don't miss this powerful book. You will never regret it."

—STACEY GENTRY LINDSEY, National Vice President, Arbonne International; Founder, They Serve 2

EXCEPTIONAL
EVERY
DAY

An Empowering Process *to*
Unlock Your Why *and* Transform Your Life

EXCEPTIONAL
EVERY
DAY

JASON VALADÃO, M.D.

GREENLEAF
BOOK GROUP PRESS

This book is intended as a reference volume only. It is sold with the understanding that the publisher and author are not engaged in rendering any professional services. The information given here is designed to help you make informed decisions. If you suspect that you have a problem that might require professional treatment or advice, you should seek competent help.
Neither the Department of the Navy nor any other component of the Department of Defense has approved, endorsed, or authorized this product.

Published by Greenleaf Book Group Press
Austin, Texas
www.gbgpress.com

Distributed by Greenleaf Book Group

For ordering information or special discounts for bulk purchases, please contact Greenleaf Book Group at PO Box 91869, Austin, TX 78709, 512.891.6100.

Design and composition by Greenleaf Book Group
Cover design by Greenleaf Book Group
Cover: clock image copyright Vector House, 2018. Used under license from Shutterstock.com

Publisher's Cataloging-in-Publication data is available.

Print ISBN: 978-1-62634-607-9

eBook ISBN: 978-1-62634-608-6

Part of the Tree Neutral® program, which offsets the number of trees consumed in the production and printing of this book by taking proactive steps, such as planting trees in direct proportion to the number of trees used: www.treeneutral.com

Printed in the United States of America on acid-free paper

19 20 21 22 23 24 25   10 9 8 7 6 5 4 3 2 1

First Edition

This book is dedicated to all the sons and daughters

lost to the fog of war. These sacrifices are the greatest

gifts a country could ever receive.

"Most people think that when they acquire wealth, success, getting the biggest house, starting the fastest-growing company, marrying the prettiest wife, making the Forbes list, whatever, they think that's going to transform them. They think the heavens are going to open, the angels are going to sing, euphoria's going to happen, and all their worries will just disappear. But that's not how it goes. It's anticlimactic. All of that, it doesn't change anything. The meaning of life is in the process. It's all in the process, and in my case it's my commitment to add value any time I interact with anybody. If you can get that in alignment, find a way to help someone else while you help yourself, then everything else flows."

—Jay Abraham

CONTENTS

FOREWORD

"Hello, sir. Thank you for your work. I'm Jason Valadão, and I'm wondering how I might join the faculty for this program. This is what I want to do!"

Thus began my introduction to Jason Valadão and my first experience with Jason living out what he calls The Process.

"Thank you for your interest Jason. Let's see how you feel about the program when we regather in three months, and if you're still interested, we can talk," I replied. This wasn't the first time someone had made such a request, and none had ever followed up.

But none of them was Jason Valadão, and apparently none of them were connected to their Process; knowing and living out their "why" every day. Discouragement is not in the vocabulary for those who are traveling The Process journey.

Three months later, there he was again; "Hello, sir. I've not forgotten our conversation, and I'm convinced more than ever this is something I want to do."

This exchange led to Jason becoming the first "Fellow" for the American Academy of Family Physicians Chief Resident Leadership Development Program, a year long program that has helped catalyze the leadership development of over 5,000 emerging physician leaders. More importantly, a friendship was born for me with one of the most remarkable men I have ever known.

It was Robert Greenleaf, a man who is credited with having started the modern Servant Leadership movement and founded the

Greenleaf Center for Servant Leadership, who once wrote: "The means justifies the ends," and in doing so turned conventional wisdom on its head.

I've never met anyone who exemplifies this idea more than Jason. His life story is in and of itself unlike anything I've ever heard, and that alone would make Jason remarkable. But it is who he has become not only in spite of his story, but in many ways because of it that makes Jason truly remarkable. His life demonstrates that being "exceptional every day" is not only possible, but that it happens because of a deliberate approach to living, grounded in meaning and service to others.

When Jason writes, "I want to help people live better, healthier, and more productive lives," this is not a tag line or quaint life mission statement. It is the reason Jason gets up every morning (quite early!), ready to engage fully with life.

It is my privilege to introduce you to Jason Valadão. If your experience is anything like mine has been, your life will never be the same, and you'll never miss the life you leave behind. Welcome to The Process.

—*Mark H. Greenawald, M.D.*
Vice Chair for Academic Affairs and Professional Development
Carilion Clinic Department of Family
and Community Medicine
Associate Professor of Family Medicine, Virginia Tech Carilion
School of Medicine, Roanoke, VA

INTRODUCTION

". . . [Y]ou will not find a single new principle; every one of them is as old as civilization; yet you will find but few people who seem to understand how to apply them."
—Napoleon Hill

86,400 SECONDS AND COUNTING

I am so glad you're here and that you've decided to go on this journey with me. I want you to know that this is not just any old book sitting on the shelf or downloaded to your tablet. If used properly, *Exceptional Every Day* is a vehicle to where you want to go with your life. From the 86,400 seconds spanning the next twenty-four hours to the days and nights ahead, your journey will be anything but boring.

I began writing my life's screenplay and gathering together its actors (me and everyone who would come into my life) many years ago. It all started when I was sixteen, parked every night next to that big blue sea on the coast of Northern California, in the cab of my pickup truck, where I rocked myself to sleep.

You see, I'd left home on May 1, 1996, after finally having it out with my father.

At the time, my life was full of pain and suffering, food stamps and government cheese, and neglect and shame. To friends and outsiders, our household might have looked like a normal family, but they didn't have any real sense of what was going on behind closed doors. From not enough food to too much drinking and all the yelling . . . it's still painful to think back on those times. Sure, some love was mixed in, but it was generally superficial—nothing too deep or with any real emotion.

After my father stood up from the couch and beat me to a pulp, I decided to leave for good. It was near the end of my junior year of high school and, having no place to go, I lived in my truck. In a small coastal town of around five thousand people, yes, everyone knew. I was fortunate to have a job, some money, and still attend school. I even stayed on as captain of the varsity basketball team, finishing up my junior year of high school and maintaining nearly a 4.0 GPA.

I never looked back.

THE PROCESS

During those lonely nights in my truck, I began thinking about how I wanted to manage my life. I started focusing on how to transcend my birthright, move past my parents' life, and accomplish something more—a whole lot more. When I eventually put these thoughts on paper, one phrase kept coming up, page after page, this thing I decided to call "The Process." I wanted to be a doctor, so I was thinking scientifically; cells in the body, organs—even bridges, cities, and all sorts of other things around us—develop through a process. While I understood this engineering, I'd never heard anyone apply a similar concept to their purpose in life.

As a young child, and then even more often as a teenager, people would ask, "What do you want to be when you grow up?" I'd give my best answer and get a reply such as, "But why would you want to do that?"

This exchange happened more than once. People seemed to think I was destined to be a fisherman (like my maternal grandfather and uncle), logger (like many of the fathers in my town), or janitor (like my own father, uncle, aunt, and most of the Portuguese side of my family). Any of those jobs would've been fine, but none would have defined me as a person. I wanted to figure out this thing I came to call The Process, to discover myself and create the life I wanted instead of losing who I was in others' preconceived paths.

Unlike a bowl of instant oatmeal or a cup of noodles, The Process isn't instantaneously done. With no direct path to my ultimate goals or purpose, it would be a journey. I knew I wanted to help people. And I knew that being a physician was a great way to do so, and I believed I could do it. Even after one of my high school teachers, someone I really looked up to, told me I was throwing my life away and would likely never get a college education.

Maybe you've been told something like this. Maybe you've walked a similar path; maybe, just maybe, you're on that journey right now. If so, the journey I'm about to share will help you realize that the destination is only what you make of it. Though everyone gets addicted to the destination, what we need to be doing is appreciating and trusting this process. The journey, or more appropriately, The Process, is what brings the desired joy.

MY WHY

You probably have lots of questions. I'm talking about this Process thing, yet you have no real idea about who I am (unless you're someone who happened to stumble upon my blog). That's because it took awhile to garner the courage to put pen to paper and share my story. I don't think of myself as special; I'm just this guy with a weird conviction to do whatever I can to help people get better every day.

Yes, that is what I truly care about—my Why. I didn't have someone to look to for guidance. I didn't have any role models who could steer me in the right direction; my parents, perhaps like yours, were just trying to put food on the table, and my overwhelmed high school guidance counselors focused on a select group of students. However, I innately knew that, if I could, it was my duty to help others like me. This compulsion to prevent those who were suffering from repeating my story was—and is—my Why.

Refining my Why has taken some time. I lost track here and there as I pursued those things society labels as important: degrees, awards, prestige, and money. I'm sure if you look at your own life, you'll be able to add some other items to this list.

My closest friends and family members know I didn't get too crazy during this time. I stayed away from drugs, alcohol, and gambling (being the designated driver or wingman suited me just fine), but I still made lots of mistakes. For various reasons, my real dreams were on hold—from total ignorance about the talent required to make it to the NBA to the cost of medical school and what I would do if, by chance, plans didn't work out. All those notes I'd made about my dreams and The Process were stored in a small plastic box at my grandmother's home while I went away to school.

So, there I am: the son of two immigrant parents, a boy who ran away from home at sixteen and went on to college to study medicine. After some great career fair advertising, my roommate and I decided the military might be a good thing. In 2000, not much was going on in terms of wars, so we figured we'd serve for a few years, earn some money for graduate school, and go from there. I would have plenty of time to discover my underlying purpose (or so I thought).

After years of training, I became a glorified copilot during the Iraq and Afghanistan invasions. Then, I was a naval science instructor at the University of California Berkeley. I got married; I volunteered as a mentor to aspiring young men, many from broken homes who'd experienced daily violence at their doorsteps. I also learned a lot about football. During this time at UC Berkeley, people kept crossing my path and sharing ideas that coalesced into a special inspirational potion. My Process reawakened and found new life.

Once again, I was thinking about becoming a doctor. Ten years of military service had passed right before my eyes. My medical school entrance exam scores were no longer good, so a lot of work lay ahead. The idea was there but The Process needed finessing.

When I decided to apply to medical school, my life was a mess. I was busy, working about forty hours a week, and studying, halfway through a master's degree. There had been setbacks. The Blue Angels flight demonstration squadron had rejected my application. My father had suffered a short but extremely painful battle with cancer and recently passed away, and I was getting over some chemotherapy and radiation treatment of my own (I know you want to learn more about my experience with cancer but trust me, this is a story for another time). From the outside, it appeared I was managing rather well. On the inside, however, being a husband, a good listener, and a good person seemed impossible. My heart felt like it was being ripped out.

The Process, however, gave me hope. Once underway, I was sure things would get better. I trusted that, with time and continued effort, I would fully live out my life's purpose.

YOUR PROCESS

Some of you are eager to get started. I can sense your pulse, hammering somewhere between a brisk walk and light jog. That's great, because keeping that heart rate up with things that excite you—exercise, an adventure, a good book—will increase your odds of living a longer, more fruitful life. And I'm here to give you the underground, hush-hush, classified scoop on what The Process means and how it can help manage your life.

Some of you may be chuckling or rolling your eyes. I get it. You've scoured the bookshelves, seen all the treatises on time management, and are, quite frankly, tired. Who wants to waste another minute reading or listening to some person who thinks he has it all figured out? If you're feeling any of this right now, I'd like to entice you with just a few words: Appreciate The Process—*your* Process.

We're about to go on a journey that will align your priorities with your everyday life. A journey to help not only to envision the things you want out of life but also realize them. We cannot sit on the couch and slow time; life doesn't work that way. Instead, we must actively take hold of what we've been given. What we do with time makes it one of life's most valuable commodities.

If you manage it well, time will become an amazing asset. To do this, however, you *must* understand *your* Process—not my Process, or your mother's, father's, or coworker's, but one of your very own.

A long time ago, I learned that connecting with people demands we must under promise and over deliver. The opposite gets us nowhere. Now, there may be parts of the following chapters where you don't agree with what I've written, and that is one of the beautiful parts of The Process. You don't need to always agree with me. I want you to ask tough questions because it's those very questions that will truly help you on your journey.

Exceptional Every Day will reveal how changing a few habits can create a more productive, more efficient, and, of course, more rested and joyful *you*. Life management—finding more time to live the life that excites you—is what we are after with The Process. Are you willing to risk a few hours of your time? If you are ready to reap the benefits of the life you desire, then why wait? Here's a front-row seat to The Process and a better tomorrow.

HOW THIS BOOK IS ARRANGED

Now that you've learned a little bit about me and my reasons for wanting to help you succeed, let me introduce you to the method behind finding your Process. As we progress from chapter to chapter, I'll be preparing you for the adventure ahead. It doesn't matter what happened in the past because the present and the future are yours to be lived.

The chapters of this book are arranged by what I have come to understand as the basic priorities of life. Look, what I've outlined will not match up perfectly with everyone's priorities, but I believe that each of us shares certain foundations. As you progress through this book, learning and understanding new concepts, you may need to sprinkle a priority here or there. This individualization is exactly what The Process is all about.

In Chapter 1, I'll help you realize and accept that *you* are the most important priority in your life. Without *you*, there's nothing to give to others.

Once we've established your self-awareness and self-leadership capabilities, we'll transition into Chapters 2 and 3, where you'll begin to comprehend that your own personal Why will drive the success you desire.

After embracing a renewed sense of self and purpose, Chapter 4 examines the home—what I like to call your Daily Table. While your number one priority is you, we'll discover the importance of that halo surrounding your epicenter and how there is no such thing as a self-made man or woman.

Chapter 5, where I will enable you to see how work and passion connect, is a critical juncture. This is where The Process truly comes to life, because our passion (and, hopefully, our work) inspires and motivates us daily. At this point, the lens you've been looking through will be less cluttered; you'll have gained perception and acuity, which results in an improved vision of who you are and who you want to become. And then, in Chapter 6, I'll throw in those little critters—namely, unhealthy relationships you've bred, watered, and restored along the way—that always seem to burrow into our lives.

Now, you need to trust that these chapters are arranged in this order because I believe they apply to all of us. This brings us to Chapter 7, which is about the fundamentals of existence: body, mind, food, and health—and all the ways each of us can improve these for the better. From the physical, we move to Chapter 8's investigation of spirituality (your faith base or higher being: call it what you will).

Who doesn't enjoy rest, play, sex, and sleep? Chapter 9, then, might just become a favorite as we explore the necessity for these activities. Then Chapter 10 urges a deeper look at your calling, an examination of how you may be drawn to accomplish something bigger.

In Chapter 11, I'll share some real-life examples as we take everything learned thus far and distill the best way to grasp The Process. And finally, in Chapter 12, I will root you in The Process. Once you've completed all twelve chapters, it will be your turn to apply your Process so you can live out the life you've been eager to achieve all along.

1 IT HAS TO BE ABOUT YOU

"The question is not what you look at, but what you see."
—Henry David Thoreau

GETTING STARTED

It's time to begin this journey. I want to start off with a sincere "thank you." Because I wasn't popular, because I came from a "mixed" family, many people never gave me a chance in life. But you have already taken some time to learn a little bit about me and my conviction regarding this inspiring thing I call The Process. Because of your willingness to learn more, my message can spread. The best thing about my message? It starts with you. Yes, *you*.

If you're like me, life to this point hasn't really been about *you*; it's been more about all the people and things that *need* you. Though that's not necessarily a bad thing, everyone should understand they matter. Each of us must recognize our uniqueness and then make nurturing that sense of self a top priority. It's far from selfish to love ourselves; that's what enables us to go above and beyond, to grow. For many years, I failed to appreciate my unique self and, consequently, missed out on many wonderful things. There's no reason for you to do the same; there's no reason to continue that path.

Caring about ourselves, recognizing our strengths and weaknesses, and choosing to become better are some of the most selfless daily acts we can ever commit. From an early age, many of us have been told through words or actions that "you don't matter." That we were brought into this world "by accident," or we're "in the way," or "there's no way" we could become this or that.

Others may have had what appeared to be the greatest support system ever. Sports, music lessons, the best private schools—activities thrust upon these children before they could even write legibly. Perhaps you're somewhere in the middle; our backgrounds are not always black and white but often full of gray. Some of us received an occasional pat on the back before, only seconds later, being compared unfavorably to a brother or sister, making us feel our abilities and accomplishments weren't good enough. Maybe you were spoiled as a child, lavished with material goods by your parents, but now, as an adult, lack any real connection because your choices failed to meet Mom and Dad's expectations.

Did you experience one of these beginnings? If you look around, you'll certainly observe many who bought into a lifetime of "I don't matter." Without proper guidance, these people will struggle to work through The Process. To understand all The Process entails, you must reject "I don't matter" and embrace "I matter," because The Process is anything and everything that makes you who you are. The Process is *you*.

You miss out on all the amazing things right in front of you when your focus is on what isn't good enough or, as my father used to say, being "a day late and a dollar short." Reading *Exceptional Every Day* and exploring The Process—along with everything else you are doing to become your best self—means you're discrediting that negative notion, eliminating "never good enough" from your vocabulary, and beginning to thrive.

THE PROCESS: HISTORICAL AND PRESENT-DAY EXAMPLES

You know all those vehicles you see on the road today? I'd like to share an abridged story of the mind behind those autos. That mind belonged to Henry Ford. You see, when Mr. Ford was just a kid, he decided he didn't want to work on the family farm. Rather than be subjected to the harsh realities of farm labor (the way his siblings were), he persuaded his parents to allow him to remain in the house to study and tool around with various projects. Mr. Ford was adamant in his efforts, and the result was a direct reflection of his belief in and valuation of himself; he knew he mattered; he found his Process. Eventually, Mr. Ford left home, worked his way into the engineering world, and transcended current ideas of transportation to invent the first automobile. What you see today on the streets and highways around you is a physical manifestation of one man's belief in himself.

Henry Ford isn't the only successful person to use The Process. Here's another story, one of a young boy named Barry, who was raised by his mother and grandparents on an island in the Pacific Ocean. His darker skin made him wonder where he'd come from; his personal sense of self lay somewhere between confusion and investigation. Whether due to the love he'd received or from genetic imprinting at conception, Barry gravitated toward one of this century's greatest achievements. From the islands of Hawaii and Indonesia to some of the finest universities in North America, Barry eclipsed limitations to become the forty-fourth president of the United States. You know him as Barack Obama.

Whether you're a fan of President Obama or not, it's hard to discredit his achievement. He truly believed in what I call The Priority of Self. Without such conviction, young Barry and the road he paved would not have withstood one of man's most harrowing natural disasters—being judged and criticized by another human being.

The United States had never elected a president who was not Caucasian, and this change upset some citizens and made them uncomfortable. President Obama was often demeaned and discredited simply because of the color of his skin. Despite his past work as senator for the state of Illinois, nothing seemed to be good enough. There were even people in politics and business who questioned his citizenship.

Unlike any politician before him, President Obama appeared before the guillotine daily, watching his every step and move. This constant scrutiny, in fact, made President Obama a Process trailblazer. He tore down walls; for the first time, many struggling souls saw themselves as valuable human beings. Many people continue to be inspired by his example today.

Famous people aren't the only ones who can demonstrate how focusing on ourselves must be a priority. Think about your coworkers. Or schoolmates. Or perhaps the neighbor who's out walking her dog every night. Everybody with a capable mind should embody that fundamental daily concept: the person staring back from the mirror is The Priority.

The reality, however, is that most of us are doing the exact opposite.

LOSING FOCUS

Consider your friend, the guy who drinks most nights of the week, stays up late watching movies, and then tells you how much his life sucks. Perhaps some obstacle in his path caused him to lose sight of what matters in life. However he got there, this person has succumbed to negativity and embraced a passive mindset.

Or what about the relative who doesn't have time to exercise? She's decided there are just too many more important priorities on her list of things to do. This is a common problem; people like her have fallen prey to "there's not enough time." This thinking discredits the physical and mental benefits to health or distorts the amount of time involved in exercise. Often, there are other reasons: she can't afford a gym membership or doesn't like sweating and feeling dirty.

The list of excuses could go on forever.

There are many reasons we drift and lose focus. Some are as simple as not knowing how to say "no" to friends and family or employers. Requests from friends start piling up; the boss has asked you to stay late multiple times. Now you're missing out on life's joys, such as attending a child's school activity, cultivating the garden, eating meals with your family, or taking thirty minutes each day to read a good book. These obligations creep up and illustrate how often we are unaware and how much we undervalue ourselves. I've been there (and am often still in that position), and this loss of focus on The Priority has kept me from being the best *me* possible.

Because we tend to undervalue ourselves, it's crucial to develop our own sense of self. Not necessarily what our life's purpose is (that comes later, I promise), but rather *who we really are*. Each of us is more than the exterior reflected in the mirror. We're more than—and better than—some of the words buzzing through our lips. Each of us is more than our daily actions and, more importantly, reactions. In fact, none of these should confine us but instead propel us toward a richer understanding of who we are and what we seek to become. My friends, to get to this deep understanding and acceptance, we must continue to follow The Process. As motivational author Napoleon Hill said, "You can do it if you believe you can."

THE IMPORTANCE OF BEING SELF-AWARE

Few professional people possess a higher sense of self-awareness than Napoleon Hill, the author of *Think and Grow Rich*, one of the twentieth century's best-selling self-development books. Mr. Hill studied notable people to identify his philosophy of success, and he was fortunate to have worked with Andrew Carnegie and J.D. Rockefeller, some of the richest and most innovative men of his era.

Why doesn't everyone achieve this same level of success and wealth? Much, I believe, is due to our educational system and its surrounding values and priorities. Teachers aren't really at fault for student failures in self-realization; it's the system. For the past one hundred years, education has focused on literature, math, science, engineering, and myriad other subjects. Where are the courses on self-awareness? If studies aimed at self-realization were introduced in high school and offered again in college, more people would be working The Process and doing amazing things, like Mr. Hill, Mr. Carnegie, and Mr. Rockefeller.

What about women? Unfortunately, women in the late 1800s and early 1900s were not provided the same freedoms as men, or I believe Mr. Hill would have been compelled to study their actions and ideas, too. Today, you'll see that more women than men maintain a pure sense of self and commit far fewer acts of violence, indiscretion, or self-harm.

Over the past thirty years, one woman has stood out in demonstrating a great sense of self-awareness and success, and I believe that woman is none other than Oprah Winfrey. Some may see Ms. Winfrey as a polarizing figure, thanks to the national reactions she conjures with a single comment, book review, or interview. From book club to movies, from television talk shows to production enterprises, Ms. Winfrey has used her various business platforms to craft the curriculum for those who seek to do and become more. She didn't start out rich—there was no large bank account or family assets to fund her future—but from an early age, Ms. Winfrey possessed something much more important: a mindset oriented toward growth and abundance. That mindset ultimately allowed her to brilliantly manage her life, despite several enduring obstacles.

Ms. Winfrey believed in herself. She also believed in prioritizing and aggressively and continually pursuing the refinement of any qualities limiting her potential. This ongoing journey was predicated on self-awareness. She wasn't blind to her faults; on the contrary, Ms. Winfrey was rather attentive to and inspired by them. In the process of growth, she constructed a platform for personal betterment that would not only give hope to the oppressed but also change lives.

Thank you, Oprah Winfrey, for establishing the value of making *me* a top priority. When I—and everyone else—recognize The Priority, it's possible to do so much more than the world had previously destined.

People like Oprah Winfrey are all around us. Perhaps they lack her name recognition, but all share a similar persistence of the belief in self. Fundamentally and importantly, self-aware people know themselves. Whether good or bad times, they must be willing to evaluate without batting an eye, without playing the fool. Joining the ranks of the self-aware is an undertaking. Learning to examine yourself critically and reflectively takes energy and time; you may need to give other things up to get to that point, but you will soon see the value in doing so. After all, finding yourself is your top priority, and developing self-awareness is a key step in that Process. Through that, you will come to appreciate the experiences and victories the future will undoubtedly provide.

Are you ready?

SELF-LEADERSHIP

Before we finish this section on the importance of self-awareness, I want to introduce you to a relatively new twist—self-leadership.

Have you heard of this before? The concept of self-leadership isn't well illustrated, as you might imagine from the amount of people who are struggling in their daily lives (perhaps in this very moment *you* are feeling life's toll, too).

While self-awareness and self-leadership go hand in hand, they are unique and different. It is one thing to be aware of who you are and know your priorities; it's a completely different matter to adhere to your priorities and make the right decisions. If you're willing to invest time, money, and resources in your most appreciable asset—*you*—then self-leadership is quite a simple process. But we know that, for most people, such an investment can be hard to make.

I like to call self-leadership "appreciable." Self-leadership is not like a new car, which depreciates in value the minute you turn the ignition and drive off the lot. No; with every step in the direction toward self-leadership, you gain value (appreciate). Sure—life's hiccups, setbacks, and roadblocks (whatever names you want to give these facets of life we must contend with) will, of course, occur. But you can lead yourself right out of those events. Any work put into self-leadership will be worth the investment. In fact, that appreciation of self will be much more valuable than any compounding interest gained from long-term financial investments.

Leading and investing in yourself make you become successful and significant. You'll be able to affect so many others. You'll live the life you were destined to live, and this is why the self-leadership part of your Process—a foundation you cannot live without—is critical. You cannot be a follower; you must *lead* your life. Leading means making quick decisions when needed, without vacillating or procrastinating on important issues. People who refuse to make decisions, even in matters of the smallest significance, will never achieve what they truly desire.

As we strive to increase our self-awareness and self-leadership, one of the best strategies to implement is looking to the example of those who are doing it better, brighter, and more attentively.

Without a strong sense of who you are, evading obstacles and managing your life will be challenging. But don't worry—your Process has only begun. And trust me: it's worth every step.

SELF-CONTROL

Let's revisit author Napoleon Hill. Almost one hundred years ago, Mr. Hill wrote about self-control in his classic, *The Law of Success*.[1] He identified self-control as the guiding purpose of this book, that managing life cannot be accomplished without first having (or at least working toward) this discipline. That's because when you master self-control (a concept I'm still working on), you'll be the grand champion of your life. Just think about what self-control means, and you'll soon see how priceless it is. I don't believe you can make a better investment, as the return on the investment made in mastering self-control will far exceed any endeavor you have or ever will embark upon.

While Mr. Hill's segment on self-control spanned more than forty pages, the entire book is one big treatise on the subject. From having a purpose to developing self-confidence, from saving money and cultivating enthusiasm to dealing with failure, each lesson in *The Law of Success* includes a silver lining. Having read this book several times, I'm certain that self-control is by far the most important character trait when it comes to living a successful life.

What, exactly, is self-control? Unfortunately, we rarely answer this question with a clear or unified voice. Rules are in place for those who commit crimes (breaking the law thus proving these people lack self-control). Children who don't obey are scolded. Bad lifestyle choices lead to paying the ultimate price; as a medical doctor, I've seen how poor health is due to patients' undesirable food and

---

1   Napoleon Hill, *The Law of Success: Deluxe Edition* (New York: First Tarcher Perigree reprint, 2017).

exercise choices. Outcome-based examples of self-control abound, but the idea and concept lack one simple definition.

Look around and you'll see lessons on self-control everywhere: a customer yelling at the clerk; the CEO who acts one way at the office and another completely different way at home; military commanding officers fired for failure to lead properly; you and me, consciously deciding that one more bad choice isn't a big deal.

Here's my challenge to you—examine what self-control means to you and how this trait could become your greatest asset. When you figure out a few things, keep looking; this review is a process that will surely never end. Don't fret over one bad choice or a lacking essential quality. The Process is about improvement, not the need to prove anything in the moment.

Every action is based upon our ability to foster self-control, and nothing appears to be more important than mind control. Start with your thoughts; by mastering these, you'll surely be ready for the adventure that awaits on your journey through The Process.

As we move into the next section, I want to leave you with some thought-provoking lines from Mr. Hill's great work—lines we can use to challenge ourselves daily:

> A person with well-developed *self-control* does not indulge in hatred, envy, jealously, revenge or any similar destructive emotions. A person with well-developed *self-control* does not go into ecstasies or become ungovernably enthusiastic over anything or anybody. Greed and selfishness and self-approval beyond the point of accurate self-analysis and appreciation of one's actual merits, indicate lack of *self-control* in one of its most dangerous forms.[2]

---

2   Hill, *Law of Success*, p. 355.

LOSING YOUR SENSE OF SELF:
THE CHRIS DORNER STORY (PART I)

Most would agree that rough patches—confusion about who we are, times when we don't really know ourselves—are common. These roadblocks consequently cause us to falter and stumble. Because we're unsure of ourselves, peer pressure becomes the reality and creates a domino effect of one bad decision after another.

None of us should suffer from this confusion. We must, therefore, make learning our dislikes, likes, desires, aspirations, and ability to discern fulfillment from simple pleasure a priority.

In that spirit, I want to tell you about my friend, Chris Dorner. Our friendship began with a handshake and developed rather quickly—about as fast as a packet of instant oatmeal becomes breakfast.

We met in 2001 after I'd completed the Navy's Officer Candidate School (OCS), part of my preparation for military service. OCS was thirteen weeks of nonstop chaos. From the moment I stepped out of the taxi and grabbed my bag from the trunk, I was barraged with demands from Marine Corps drill instructors. Within seconds, I was ordered to remove my shoelaces and put them back in again, over and over, for what felt like an hour, while my every move was scrutinized. Nervous and scared—at the ripe old age of twenty-one—what an understatement for how I felt that day! But I made it through OCS.

After graduating from OCS, I flew back to California for a couple of months while I awaited flight training. I was assigned to work in a recruiting office in Southern California. On my second or third day there, in walked a fit, approximately 225-pound African American man who looked like the rapper LL Cool J mixed with Michael Clarke Duncan, the actor. This was Chris Dorner, who would become my friend. He'd applied to join the Navy and was waiting for a waiver for a knee injury sustained when he'd played college football. As the recruiting officer, I was responsible for processing his final paperwork.

As I reviewed Chris's personal statement and application, his passion about service became apparent. Raised by a single mother, at about the age of twelve, he'd joined the Los Angeles Police Department's Junior Cadet Program and dreamed of being a Los Angeles Police Department (LAPD) officer one day. The program brought him the masculine attention he so desperately wanted.

From the beginning, I saw qualities in Chris I wanted to cultivate in myself: self-confidence, strength, and a defined purpose—he wanted to be of service to others. Chris had a good sense of self, something I believe is so critical to a well-lived life. Though I returned to Pensacola around the end of 2001, we stayed in touch; in early 2002, when Chris's application was approved and he was assigned to an OCS class, I picked him up at the airport. As the years went by, our friendship grew—and I saw that Chris maintained his sense of self better than most. Through good times and bad, he found a way to keep his priorities straight.

After successfully completing OCS, Chris was awarded the opportunity to go to flight school. The sky would truly be his limit. During primary flight training at Vance Air Force Base in Enid, Oklahoma, he and a classmate stumbled upon a bag of money—approximately $8,000—on the side of a very quiet highway. No one was around—no cars, people, or cameras in sight. Just two young officers with a decision to make. And they did the right thing; they went to the authorities and the money was returned to the church that had lost it.

A few months later, Chris began to struggle in flight school. Talking on radios, adjusting flight controls, and maintaining situational awareness (all at the same time) weren't working out for him. Now, Chris wasn't an anomaly; this happens to many adventurous souls. I could see he wasn't grasping The Process involved with each essential step. He didn't give up, however. Chris realized he needed a change, so he went to work in the administration office.

Eventually, Chris would transition into the U.S. Naval Reserves, where he would become an intelligence officer. And during this time, he began to chase after that childhood dream of becoming an LAPD officer. Chris was finally getting the chance to be who he'd always wanted to be.

I was there on March 3, 2006, when Chris graduated from the LAPD Academy, less than four years after he'd started flight school. Chris was beaming, his smile infectious. Looking on with pride were his mother, sister, and girlfriend. And me; I was extremely proud of my friend, as I stood there in my uniform, supported by crutches after having surgery for a ruptured Achilles tendon earlier that morning. There was no way I would miss this event. Chris and I posed together as my wife took a photo; little did we realize that, almost exactly seven years later, that same picture would be all over the internet, on CNN, Fox, ABC, and every other news channel imaginable. Not because of something heroic or honorable but because of something horrific. During those seven years, Chris unfortunately lost that sense of self that had previously guided him so successfully. This loss led to death and broken hearts for innocent people and their families—people who will never be the same. In the pursuit of service, Chris had forgotten about himself and who he was.

I know—you're wondering what happened to Chris. I promise we'll return to his story in Chapter 2. But for now, I want you to understand how important the power of knowing yourself is. And how significant *not knowing* yourself can be; it's not just a minor inconvenience. It can be tragic. Chris's example of not knowing—of losing—himself is extreme, but I believe it paints the proper picture. There's a reason why this is the top priority in your Process: everything starts with *you*.

Go to the closest mirror right now and take a look at yourself; you cannot hide from yourself, nor should you want to. Getting to truly and deeply know *who you are*, beyond the superficial image, may be a challenge. However, you are already on the path to becoming more self-aware, and Chris's example has illustrated how truly destructive not knowing yourself can be. What follows will surely narrow the gap between the self you think you know and the true *you* The Process will uncover.

GOALS AND FULFILLMENT

I recently spoke to a group of approximately five hundred high school students and was amazed by their general lack of commitment. While they spoke highly of going to college or joining the military or finding a job, very few had set actual goals, let alone envisioned their futures. I asked some questions about vision, the meaning of joy in their lives, and belief in themselves and their abilities. Judging by the number of hands that went up, I'd say fewer than ten percent understood the meaning of fulfillment; only about five percent bought into the notion of setting specific, obtainable goals. This was so hard for me to comprehend—I'd lived my life 180 degrees in the other direction. But I also realized that lack of understanding wasn't all their fault. Perhaps these young people had absorbed these things without realizing their value. For many students, life might be about getting through the day and hoping they'd live to see the next one. In such a scenario, when the top priority is survival, focusing on yourself is typically an afterthought.

No one can know themselves without grasping two things: where you stand today and where you want to step tomorrow. That vision for the future is most important; it's the ability to see through the window of despair and stagnation that often comes our way to a new set of circumstances. This sense of being able to look with a new and enlightening perspective encompasses our sense of self. All of us have hopes and dreams, but most fail to put the necessary pieces in place to make these a reality. And that situation creates a perfect environment for The Process, and when The Process can flourish, great achievements in life can happen.

Charles de Gaulle, a former French Army general and president of France, is remembered for saying, "History does not teach fatalism. There are moments when the will of a handful of free men breaks through determinism and opens up new roads. People get the history they deserve."

At this stage of The Process, breaking through is necessary. Forward motion cannot happen without planning. It is here, in the ability to consider a future, that we can appreciate the power of goals in establishing and pursuing the person we hope to become. By setting goals, we stand ready to welcome the future, beckoning experiences sure to come our way. Once a sense of ambition and an objective to be met have been cultivated, we can better focus on the top priority—knowing and transforming yourself into the best *you* possible.

True fulfillment is gained through knowing ourselves while pursuing personal goals. After all, anticipation of success is often sweeter than the actual attainment of a goal. That's because true joy comes from the various steps taken along the way, including the heartbreaks, roadblocks, big wins, and close losses. While it's great to achieve success, it is through these everyday experiences that we accept how anticipation and pursuit of the goal are as fundamental to happiness as achievement. Welcoming this joy is the heart of The Process.

HAVING A MENTOR OR COACH TO HELP BRING OUT YOUR TRUE SELF

Simon Sinek, author of *Start with Why*, once said, "A mentor is not someone who walks ahead of us to show us how they did it. A mentor walks alongside us to show us what we can do." Finding a mentor, no matter how old or at what stage of life you are, can benefit you in so many ways. When it comes to self-development, a mentor or coach is truly key; listening to others helps us gain and maintain perspective, knowledge, and ultimately wisdom. I'd say that finding a mentor is not merely a priority; that would be a true understatement of mentoring's value. I wholeheartedly contend that working with a mentor is essential. Why? Ask most people who've truly "made it" and I'd bet they'd proclaim how valuable a teacher, coach, or mentor had been in their lives. Anything becomes a priority when the received value is realized.

If a utility tool were ever assigned to The Process, it would be a mentor. For those who've never utilized a coach or mentor, imagine having someone help you figure out (or, at the very least, define) your journey. None of us gets through life on our own; too much to do, waning resources, and barely enough time mean we need help. Let's say you're an avid reader—finishing one or two books dedicated to your personal growth and development may not provide the same powerful message as a fifteen- to twenty-minute conversation with a mentor who desires the best for you.

Looking at your reflection in the mirror has low odds of revealing what needs to be done to fix what's wrong. A reflection may not calm your anxiety or anger, but another human being's voice—whether audible or written—can do the trick, especially once you've established a relationship. People are standing by, ready to help, but how do you find them? I realize you may have a difficult time connecting, so I'll make it easy. Don't look too far. Chances are, those helpful people are in the next room or a short car ride or phone call away. Perhaps they are the missing link you've been waiting for. Trust me—there's only an upside to this transaction, and reaching out to a potential mentor is well worth the interest you're already paying. So, don't waste another second on your own. Find a mentor who'll help you navigate The Process.

END-OF-CHAPTER ASSESSMENT

Take a moment to reflect upon what you learned in this chapter. I hope you now understand how critical valuing yourself is and how much trouble inevitably arises when you don't know the true *you*. Self-awareness may be your greatest ally (if, that is, you've gone beyond the superficial, such as noticing every blemish). Self-control drives every single decision and will get you where you need—and want—to go. It will keep you focused on bettering yourself while liberally employing goals and fulfillment measures. If you can turn *you* into the most important priority, your Process will be headed in the right direction.

Questions for Reflection and Direction

I'd like to introduce you to something you'll find at the end of each chapter. As an aviator and physician, checklists have been an important part of my work. Checklists help me remember precise speed and altitude required before deploying arresting gear on final approach to an aircraft carrier and correct sequence of steps when resuscitating a newborn infant who may have swallowed too much amniotic fluid. Checklists have saved me from frustration—and even from failure. I think you'll also find these easily adaptable end-of-chapter checklists a useful tool to help you apply what you're learning as you go.

Take a moment to answer the following questions, either in the space provided or in your journal. When you're ready, I'll meet you in Chapter 2.

THE PROCESS CHECKLIST

Priority 1: You

1. Describe yourself. What do you like and dislike? (No judgments—be honest!)

_____

_____

_____

What would you like to start changing about your life right now?

_____

_____

2. What can you do to make *you* a priority?

_____

_____

3. Name three people who can help support you in this endeavor.

_____

_____

_____

4. Over the next five days, write down three things you did to make yourself a top priority.

_____

_____

_____

2 EVERYONE HAS A WHY

"There are two great days in a person's life—the day we are born and the day we discover why."
—famous adage

Is there anything more motivating and inspiring than being alive? If you consider the alternative for just a second, your soul is sure to awake, your body to become energized, and you'll get on with living. Even if you truly feel life sucks, I believe you can come out of that train of thought and move forward. Once you believe that being alive and able is the greatest gift anyone could ever receive, you likely won't look back—even in dire situations. Instead, you'll want to do more, because you'll realize you can. With this realization, you're motivated to find your own essential Why.

What is this Why? It's that spark that moves you—that thing you think about every single day. That thing you hope to make better, that special something you want to accomplish. Just thinking about your Why is enough to keep your attitude positive and provide focus for living.

Life, however, is often quite short. No one knows when their last day will fall, so everyone should spend time immersed in that *one* thing. Sure, you earn a living each day at a job; you can survive— but what are you doing to truly *live*?

I think about my one thing—living and striving to do the most good for as many people as possible—every day. Even so, I still have a lot of work to do, and I would contend that you do, too! Trying to do everything, or filling time with anything (be it the need to feel busy, earn a paycheck, appease society, or anything else), is no way to approach life or The Process. My *one thing* must be *my* thing and your *one thing* needs to be *your* thing. Digging into Why will enable us to fully understand what exactly and individually this means.

Often, I illustrate this book's principles by referencing stories of collegiate and professional athletes. Why? I've been fortunate to have close and interactive relationships with quite a few. Athletes' stories include failure, injury, financial loss, divorce . . . pretty much any- thing that implies a poor outcome. Many never truly come to grips with finding their Why. What's most compelling in many stories is how often these athletes find a way to recover from desperation.

How? By seeking help. They find someone who cares for them dearly (or cares about receiving a paycheck from them) and start on a path to recovery. Now, I'm not trying to sell you on my idea of The Process by using analogies and stories of people and things I don't know as much about. I've selected from experience to give relatable examples—how figuring out your priorities (especially what truly moves you) and finding how to live them defines The Process.

A word about some differences. I've witnessed more men than women who've failed to achieve a self-realized life. I've noticed that fewer men seem to rebound from those failures, and I have some opinions on why this occurs. In my experience, women tend to be better communicators. They don't sweat the small stuff, keep their priorities straight, and realize what really matters most. They show up, and they get the job done. Women, more often than men, let The Process play itself through—*they just get it*. Without over-thinking situations, women are more likely to allow life to happen without creating their own roadblocks. Though all people should be good listeners—hey, we have two ears and one mouth for a reason—women listen more. And for The Process to survive, listening (especially to the right things) is essential.

Men, I urge you to take these notions to heart as you read. Talk with the women in your lives, acknowledge their resilience, and then open your mind; you'll learn from them, and I can all but guarantee that your life will be better for the effort. I find it's harder to write about failure points in The Process from a female perspective. This is not necessarily a bad thing. You'll more likely come across women's stories when I provide a positive example of The Process in action.

THE IMPORTANCE OF HAVING A WHY

Lindsey Vonn's story illustrates how having a Why matters. Ms. Vonn is a downhill skiing world champion and Olympic gold medalist who is one of the greatest twenty-first century athletes (male or female). She has consistently crushed it on the slopes, destroying the hopes and dreams of many of her competitors in the process. Ms. Vonn has displayed uncanny relentlessness as she's transcended her sport. She's also had her share of failures. Many tumbles down the slopes have led to many broken bones and bruises. Several times, those injuries have been described as "career ending."

Despite her injuries and setbacks, despite an inability to win every time she donned her helmet to race, Ms. Vonn kept her focus. Her enduring desire was (and is) to set an example for young athletes—especially young girls with similar aspirations—by being her best. That passion pushed her to excel on the mountain. She let nothing stand in her way of inspiring athletes everywhere. And despite those world championships and Olympic medals, Ms. Vonn is much like the rest of us. Resilience and dedication drive her Why, illustrating how aligning priorities with passion is the key to managing lives, understanding self, and putting our Why to work. That is how any of us attain true success.

LOSING YOUR WHY:
THE CHRIS DORNER STORY (PART II)

Now, think back to Chapter 1 and my friend, Chris Dorner. I'm guessing many of you searched the internet for his name; perhaps you know the rest of the story by now. But unlike the journalists and reporters who wrote those accounts, I knew the man, and my version of the story and insights into Chris's Process may be more compelling.

As I mentioned, the Chris I knew was an honorable person, a naval and police officer who was completely committed to serving others. He never appeared to be a jealous, disheartened, or inauthentic human being. But Chris forgot himself; he unconsciously distanced himself from his Purpose (the You we discussed earlier) and Why. Ultimately, Chris committed—not once, but several times—what I believe is the most heinous crime possible, taking another person's life.

On a routine patrol with his training officer, Sergeant Teresa Evans, Chris noticed two men outside a Los Angeles bank. As they stood in front of an ATM, the two appeared to be quarreling, so the officers stopped their car to investigate. Chris later told me (and stated in several court hearings) that he asked one of them what was going on but wasn't given a direct answer. Quickly realizing that the younger one was mentally ill, Chris probed a bit more and determined the two were father and son. The father eventually explained that his son was schizophrenic and homeless. Sgt. Evans began her own series of questions, but, when neither man acknowledged her, she began kicking the mentally ill individual—so many times that the man was visibly in pain. The officers left the scene, and neither mentioned the altercation to the other again.

BEGINNING OF THE END

For the next week or two, however, Chris was overcome with guilt about the incident. He couldn't sleep; emotionally distraught by what he'd witnessed, he was very uncomfortable knowing that his training officer, sworn to defend the innocent, had gotten away with a crime. Chris had sworn that same oath, and so he decided to file a report—even though he understood the department's unwritten code about "ratting out" a fellow officer and how doing so might not bode well for him.

It didn't take long for the fall-out to begin, and Chris was accused of lying. Because he'd returned from an active Naval Reserves deployment to the Middle East, Chris was on probation. That status gave little room for benefit of the doubt, much less error, and LAPD took away his badge. Chris fought to retain his status as a police officer; the legal process, however, used all the money he had plus a substantial portion of his mother's retirement savings.

The fight for what Chris believed was the truth took its toll. With little hope he'd ever see justice, Chris became enraged, depressed, and reclusive. His LAPD connection dissolved; job after job application, his efforts to re-enter civilian life were rebuffed because of the LAPD saga. As he searched for a new life, this man who'd once received a college football scholarship and been commissioned as a naval officer kept coming up empty. He was lonely, too; by 2009, Chris had cut nearly all who cared for him out of his life. While I cannot claim to know all the details, Chris's mother and sister told me that the years following his layoff from the police force were full of despair. Rejection after rejection left him hopeless, and the LAPD, he said, had ruined everything he'd ever stood for. His name was "tainted."

Upset beyond reason, Chris became delusional. He felt the attorney he'd been assigned hadn't done a good job and that corruption surrounded the entire situation. Chris believed LAPD had convinced his friends—including me—that he was a liar, and so he distanced himself from everyone. I'd asked Chris to be best man in my wedding ceremony but, because of "the situation," he wouldn't come. After the wedding, I called to check on things, but the man I'd known had changed completely. Chris even accused me of working alongside LAPD to bring him down.

Two weeks after my first child was born, in late 2009, I talked with Chris for what would be the last time. I've never stopped thinking about our conversation—he asked me to promise to stop calling, that he'd reach out when he was ready to talk again. Chris spoke with Danika for a few minutes; before we moved to Wisconsin, he said, he wanted to see the baby.

I kept my promise and ceased all communication after that call. Chris never reached out. He never met my daughter.

I wish I were making this story up. I wish I could go back in time to fix all the damage that occurred. Unfortunately, I can't. The best I can do is learn from this experience by unraveling how things for Chris—his Process—went totally awry. You see, when Chris lost his Why, he lost his way.

In those lonely, reclusive days, Chris poured his pain and depression into creating a multipage manifesto. On February 3, 2013, while most of America was enjoying Super Bowl Sunday, Chris posted his manifesto online. For Chris, that night was no celebration; it was a rampage.

A TRAGEDY UNFOLDS

I knew nothing about the two young lives ended that evening until four days later, February 7, 2013, when I received a phone call from a Los Angeles CBS News correspondent. I'd never imaged that one of my closest friends, a man who'd worn two different service uniforms, would become a murderer. Yet Chris had killed two people and was in hiding. And in that manifesto, he'd mentioned me, apologizing for missing the wedding, sorry to have argued with and distanced himself from us, and expressing his love.

Once the news broke and Chris's manifesto hit the media, the calls flooded in: from news stations (mostly in Southern California, but also from Miami, New York, and Washington, DC) and CNN's Anderson Cooper's show. Fifty to sixty calls, strangers, all leaving messages, asking about the Chris Dorner I'd known. In the immediate aftermath, these calls confused me; completely immersed in my medical school classes, I had no idea what was going on in California. And then a close friend in Orange County called—his wife had just seen Chris and me on TV, in that happy graduation celebration photo.

A classmate turned on his tablet and did a quick search. Once I had seen a few more details—that online manifesto, my name in Chris's rant, that he had not been apprehended—concern turned to fear. I called Danika and told her to head home; even though his expressions of love appeared genuine and sincere, who could be sure Chris wouldn't come after us as well? Together, Danika and I wept, in shock. Our friend had committed the most serious of crimes and there was literally nothing I could do to help him (or stop him).

The search continued; authorities set up a command post and looked for Chris in the Big Bear Mountain area of Southern California, evacuating families after his truck had been found, abandoned and aflame. Like everyone else in the nation, I was glued to my TV for news—where was Chris?

Five days later, on February 12, hundreds of families were cleared to return to their mountain homes. Jim and Karen Reynolds arrived to tidy up their rental property, less than one hundred yards away from the authorities' command post. All the homes in the adjacent area had been thoroughly searched; excluding the abandoned truck, no sign of Chris had been found. The Reynoldses had no reason to suspect anything was amiss with their cabin; they simply wanted to clean it in preparation for the upcoming ski season's next renter. Chris, however, took them by surprise, capturing the Reynoldses before tying them up, covering their heads with pillowcases, and threatening to kill them if they notified the authorities. He then took their car.

While the details of Chris's nearly weeklong stay in the cabin cannot be fully explained (the Reynoldses said there was little food in the cabin), I surmise he likely slept little and became delirious. Did he think about the mistakes he'd made? I'm certain he reflected, even if briefly, on how the LAPD incident—2008's alleged kicking incident, the report, being accused of lying, and his subsequent separation from the police force—had derailed his life's purpose. He'd already murdered innocent people, broken their family members' hearts, and left thousands on edge during the manhunt to find him.

Where was Chris headed? Knowing him as I did, it didn't seem likely he would choose to spend the rest of his life in prison, but there was no question of his guilt. I doubted he intended to take more lives, but he was certainly armed to take his own. While strangers speculated, I reflected on the man I knew. Chris had murdered because he'd been forced out of the position he so deeply cherished. Chris wanted his life and his name back. Could a man's belief in himself be so strong that he'd be willing to do whatever it took to gain what he considered justice?

A SURPRISE VISIT

It was an early weekday morning in Wisconsin and I had the morning off; even though I should've been studying for an upcoming medical school exam, I chose to spend time with our daughters, Elle (then three years old) and Siena (11 months). Time was precious, something I'd never get back, and I'd missed enough with them already, so I stayed home.

With me managing the kids, Danika headed to the gym for a morning swim. It was around 0900 in Wisconsin and she had the pool mostly to herself; when the gym manager interrupted her, Danika was startled—some people out front were waiting to see her. She needed to come immediately.

At home, I'd set the girls up to play in the living room, then taken the stairs to the basement to start a load of laundry when I heard pounding on the back door. I was worried—were Elle and Siena in trouble? Then I heard Danika yell my name. I opened the door into the kitchen and was grabbed and slammed against the wall. Within a blink of an eye, I counted seven U.S. Marshals, rifles drawn, and four large black SUVs outside, around the perimeter of our home; my wife, tears streaming down her face, begged them to put the guns away, our girls screaming in the other room. Why were they here?

The officers raided the house, room by room. They appeared to believe that, even though I hadn't contacted him in four years, our Wisconsin home might be harboring Chris, a three-hundred-pound African American man last seen in Southern California, some 2,000 miles away. Danika and I, separated in different rooms, were interrogated. Yes, I had had contact with Chris in the past; I had evidence of these limited interactions in my journal. The marshals countered with phone records.

Over the two hours our home was occupied by the marshals, we seemed to build a rapport—afterward, they helped push Danika's car out of the snow. But that friendly note could not dispel the fear I'd felt earlier; I was out of sorts. Later that day, I attended a few hours of lecture, unaware that Chris had been spotted.

When news that Chris was cornered in another cabin broke, I became glued to the TV. There, again, was the LAPD graduation photo he'd posted on Facebook. Eventually, privacy rules would cause news desks to crop the image, but my hand on his shoulder would remain, a symbol of our connection.

I learned that, not long after he'd stolen the Reynoldses' car, Chris stopped a man and commandeered his truck. After a short joy ride, he'd crashed and retreated to a different cabin, where he'd been surrounded by authorities. He wasn't going to get off the mountain.

Chris couldn't run or hide any longer. Authorities working the scene knew—as did I—Chris wouldn't let himself be caught. Using a combination of specialized equipment and basic elements, like fire, law enforcement destroyed the cabin. Did Chris shoot himself in the head or die in the fire? His driver's license, LAPD badge, and other items were found next to his body. I believe he took his life.

LEARNING FROM TRAGEDY

Watching the events unfold that day, I realized I'd lost my old friend years ago. This was not the person I once knew.

I still don't understand what happened to Chris. People I've shared this story with find it hard to believe Chris had been a good man. And I get that. My intent isn't to defend or honor Chris. Instead, I've included it to paint a picture, to show what can happen when a person loses that important and guiding Why. My old friend lost sight of his great original purpose; no Why was left in him.

Yes, Chris's story is a drastic one. But it's real.

And it's a story we can all learn from.

Could I have done something more for Chris? Could I have connected with him, helped him see the good he had within, how much he had yet to give this world? So what if LAPD said he was a liar? Why did his name—his reputation among former coworkers—mean so much to him? Was there something else? Did Chris have secrets his friends and loved ones knew nothing about? I guess I'll never know the answers to these questions. There is, however, worth in continuing to ask.

And what do we gain from this exercise? Let's start with what we know. Looking back on Chris's earlier life, we can see he'd always gone out of his way to do the right thing. He'd joined the Navy and police force because service was important to him. When he chose to stop communicating, that was the beginning of the end. I lost a great friend. And my heart goes out to all the families who, because of Chris's actions, lost their loved ones. There is no justice in any of this. Chris was outside of his body and soul when all of this happened, and that is one of the reasons I am so driven to share The Process. I know how it can help. And I know what it can prevent.

Life is all about choices. Every single day that we wake up and breathe, we make choices about the day: if we'll smile or carry a frown; if we'll lend a hand to someone in need or walk on by, as though they're invisible; if we'll leave chicken bones on someone's car (like whoever tossed theirs on my wife's windshield the other night) or place them in the trash. We decide if what someone says about our good name needs to be internalized or let go, with the wind.

In short, *we decide our Why.*

I can never get my friend back. I've accepted that he did terrible things I will never be able to comprehend. What I can do is live my Why and help other people live better every day. And that includes my sincere hope I'll help you figure out your Why so you can do the same.

END-OF-CHAPTER ASSESSMENT

Take a moment. I'd like you to breathe deeply. You deserve some time to reflect and to appreciate who and where you are in this exact moment.

Many have gone before you, and many have never made the time to reflect on their Why. Through my stories, you've seen how important finding your *one thing* is. Together, we explored just how awesome life can be *with* your Why . . . and how tragic life can be when you're *without* your Why, when you've lost your way. *Why* is more than a three-letter word incessantly used by toddlers; in our adult life, understanding Why can mean the difference between despair and inspiration, emptiness and fulfillment.

And it's my hope that you'll choose to know Why.

Questions for Reflection and Direction

Before moving on to the next chapter, take a moment to answer the questions in the space provided or in your journal. When you're ready, I'll see you in Chapter 3.

THE PROCESS CHECKLIST

Priority 2: Your Why

1. What makes you feel happy and energized? List the first three things that come to mind.

_____

_____

_____

2. Of those three things, which one feels most important?

_____

_____

_____

Write your "one thing" here.

_____

_____

_____

3. Taking your "one thing" statement, define your Why.

_____

_____

_____

4. Take a moment to think about whether you are currently living your Why. If yes, how so? If no, what is holding you back?

_____

_____

_____

3 FINDING MEANING AND INSPIRATION

"You must define your why before you can begin with the what and the how."

—Maria Reyes-McDavis

Different events and experiences lead us toward finding our Why. When pushed to the edge, some fall while others keep reaching for safety. Why is what motivates people. Some aren't compelled enough to deal with the struggle or reach for more, but I believe anyone can start embracing a growth mindset through The Process. When you do, you'll see there is an awesome journey ahead, one you'll tailor to fit *you* and no one else. Each person's Why or purpose in life is unique and important—there is no one blueprint for everyone to follow—and that's another reason finding your Why is so fun and exciting. It's designed especially for you!

When is the best time to find your Why? Is it now? Next week? Next year? Once you've gotten a degree? After you have a family? I'm going to share some good news with you. You don't have to wait for some special day—if the moment feels right, go for it! Start the exploration process and see where it takes you. You can always edit and refine your Why as you go.

FOCUS, MEANING, AND INSPIRATION BEHIND YOUR WHY

Are you afraid of death? I used to think I wasn't, but once I got married and had children, that changed. Since I was no longer accountable or responsible for just me, I became more cautious. For example, I used to jump out of perfectly good airplanes for fun; once Danika and the kids were in the picture, I quit. I wouldn't say I was ever a risk taker. Ask any of my friends and they'd likely tell you I never lived on the edge—but flying off aircraft carriers in the dark of night, especially when you're not the one in control, is hardly a forgiving occupation. Plant that aircraft carrier in the middle of a big ocean with no land in sight for thousands of miles and the situation becomes even more life threatening.

So, I'm no stranger to thinking about death. Besides taking calculated risks in the line of service, I've faced dying from cancer (though those days have passed, every cancer survivor understands the disease can always return) and witnessed impoverished villages with scores of famished souls in Africa. Those memories haunt me. But when one of my friends and former colleagues perished in a freak accident, my thoughts about risk and dying changed again. I was four weeks into writing *Exceptional Every Day* when he died, and that traumatic accident really shook me. Why, I wondered, did my friend's death shift my thinking to such an extreme?

This tragic event occurred right when I was contemplating The Process more than ever. I was in the middle of studying for a national board exam, looking for a new place to live 1,400 miles away, working my day job, raising our children, and trying to find the right words and stories to bring The Process to life. My friend's accident and death hit me with a profound realization: *The Process never stops.*

People don't physically return once they die. While traces of their unique existence remain, those memories—their smile, comforting touch, and lingering evidence of dedication—will eventually fade. With his death, I realized the worst that can happen in life is dying (and most likely, you won't even know it happens). Does that sound morbid? It seems quite clear to me that fear is fueled by the anticipation of some sort of pain combined with an important element of ignorance—not knowing what's to come.

How did this experience with death lessen my fear? I watched my friend's family and loved ones come together from near and far; I watched his squadron take care of their Marine brother. *Nothing could be more beautiful,* I thought, as fifty uniformed and sword-bearing Marines lined the corridor while the man I'd spent countless hours with was wheeled into the operating room—you see, he'd donated his organs for use in preserving others' lives. Then came the memorial service: three hundred people gathered to celebrate one who'd done so much to exemplify the military's *esprit de corps.*

However each of us connected to this tragedy, my friend had touched our lives in some special manner. He was *significant* and his priorities—his profound concept of Why—led to that climax. He'd fallen in love with being a Navy doctor of U.S. Marines and was passionate about daily service; every day, he fulfilled his Why. He knew that fear would only get in his way. While I might be sad that he is gone, how could I or anyone else regret that he'd lived his life with passion and purpose?

KEEPING THE WHY ALIVE

My first job was at Round Table Pizza. I was twelve. Based on employment laws at that time, hiring me was totally illegal but my family was poor, and I wanted to help. I bussed tables and washed dishes for $3.75 per hour, the minimum wage in 1992.

How in the world did I get that job? An inner circle of Portuguese people helped me, and I welcomed the work. It wasn't child abuse—I covered about ten to twelve hours a week, not forty—and I had fun. After only two weeks, I graduated from washing dishes and cleaning tables to making pizza. What, I wonder, would've happened had I stuck with the job through high school and college? With that drive, maybe I'd have eventually owned my own pizza chain. While I'll never know, what I do know is the experience—learning to pay attention to detail, greet patrons, and remain humble, never acting as though I were better than anyone else—shaped much of who I am today and explains how my Why came to be.

Being at the bottom of the employment food chain was the best lesson ever. During those early years, my Process was developing, and lasting impressions, formative life lessons, were made because I was motivated, inspired, and open to teaching. I may not have fully grasped why a dish had to be cleaned a certain way or the reason behind sprinkling a specific amount of mozzarella or pepperoni on each pizza, but I believed there was a reason, a specific process, behind all of it. And employing that process, in turn, had worth.

I believe that early experience has everything to do with my ability and the guidance provided within *Exceptional Every Day*, information that can help you add value to life.

THE MAKING POINT

Remember how I told you about living in my pickup truck during my junior year of high school? Most people had no idea my 1990

Chevy was both a mode of transportation and my home; for the bulk of 1996, my truck was my safe place, a haven. Would you believe I still have it? Oh, it's not as alive as it once was: the paint's peeling, undercarriage rusted throughout, tires out of alignment, hubcaps missing, and air conditioner inoperable (among other things). I'm so determined to hold on to my truck that I've repaired the interior roof cloth with staples! My daughters got a kick out of seeing me press the stapler to the sagging fabric. Whenever Elle, the oldest, asks me if she can have the truck once she has her license, I'm not sure what to tell her—I have no idea if it will last three more months, let alone the eight years before she's old enough to drive (assuming I allow it).

Why is it so hard to let go of this truck? Living in it had a profound effect, what I call a "making point" (though I'm sure those who found out would've seen my circumstances as more of a "breaking point"). I had proof that not everyone realized the positive in my situation—there was that high school economics teacher who said I was "throwing my life away" and would likely "not make it to college or ever amount to anything." No embellishment here; that's verbatim.

What that teacher said to me in 1996 struck a chord. To this day, his words have motivated me.

Today, I can forgive him for what might have been good intentions (albeit delivered in a disconcerting fashion). All he knew was the obvious, that I was living in my truck; he had no idea of the underlying situation—that my parents were divorcing and I'd been essentially left to fend for myself (working, attending school, and finding a place to live on my own). He likely had no idea—our untenable situation had been hidden from everyone in our small town, and it wasn't until my father was spotted living under a bridge that my family's true situation became apparent.

Back to my truck . . . living there allowed me to dig into myself on a new, different level. Like working at the pizza parlor, I made what was potentially a negative situation into a unique formative experience. Holding two part-time jobs, playing on a basketball team, adhering to my studies, and applying to college wasn't easy; I didn't have much time to rest or goof off. Those lonely nights in my truck, parked next to the mighty Pacific Ocean, did give me time to formulate a plan for my future. Dealing with those adversities—the pain of thinking about how much money to spend on food, clothes, gas, and eventually college—prepared me for my future bouts with cancer, the rigors of school (flight and medical), residency training, and other tragedies (like my friends' deaths). Without consciously realizing it, I'd begun to formulate my Why. I became super motivated about life and the idea of self-worth.

No one, I quickly realized, was going to solve my problems and live life for me. Without these circumstances, my making point, I wouldn't be helping you today. I owe today's successes to those nights as a sixteen-year-old sleeping in his truck.

MEETING MY MENTOR

Before I became a physician, I served as an officer in the U.S. Navy for several years. It was a lot of fun flying around in planes, fulfilling a specific purpose, executing great missions, and overcoming challenges. Bonding through squadron camaraderie, building lifelong friendships, shipping out on an aircraft carrier, growing as an officer, and developing junior personnel under my watch were valuable, rewarding, and life-shaping experiences. The Navy enabled me to see and experience parts of the country and world I'd only heard or read about. Each day, I went to work with a smile on my face; a sense of pride and motivation put spring in my step (hey, being able to practically wear pajamas—those military flight suits are pretty darn comfortable—wasn't bad, either). Even when the days were long, I was pleased with my life's direction, happy and content with my work.

People in the service call this feeling "being on the tip of the sphere," which is somewhat counterintuitive but sure makes for a cool slogan.

This journey took me from ships and flying planes to a desk and lectern. I went to the University of California Berkeley, one of the world's premier public universities, to teach and further my studies. Over those few years, I made incredible friendships, welcomed my first child, and slowly realized that my work as a naval officer, while enjoyable, was not completely aligned with my passion and purpose. I began to search for the best way to fulfill my Why, even putting my name in the hat for a spot in the coveted Blue Angels, the Navy's world-famous flight demonstration squadron. That venture went nowhere (if it had, this might be a slightly different book) but because of that rejection, more perfectly aligned—better, even—events occurred.

Fate led me to discover my Why in a very unexpected way.

It was the Christmas holiday, late in 2008, and the NCAA Emerald Bowl loomed on the horizon. I was in my second season as a volunteer coach and mentor with the UC Berkeley Golden Bears football team (also called the Cal Bears), and the team and I had arrived in San Francisco for our game against the University of Miami.

We were staying the week at the downtown Marriott when, on the second night, I met Jim Caylor. Jim was assigned to take care of the coaches' hospitality suite. We instantly connected.

Something compelled Jim to ask deep questions about my life that night. Somehow, Jim drew out things I had repressed, feelings I'd buried for no reason other than being caught up in a busy life. While I was managing within the Navy and UC Berkeley—and doing a pretty decent job of it—I wasn't necessarily following my dreams or living out my purpose. Out of sight, out of mind.

Jim asked questions I'd avoided asking myself. He wanted to know what I'd always dreamed of doing. His probing made me look at the *me* I'd been avoiding. To my amazement, Jim seemed to care more than anyone else I'd ever met, and our encounter felt even more special for its random occurrence. And then he offered me some simple advice.

That December evening, Jim and I sat in the hotel's hospitality suite, studying the beautiful San Francisco skyline. I can still hear his voice as I recall those impactful words: "Go and make copies of these books on tape; draw out a plan to study for the medical school entrance exam; take the test; get yourself into medical school; and make your original dream a reality."

Jim's words were potent. That night, he saw something that compelled him to care about me and, though I'd known Jim for only a matter of minutes, offer advice as a father would to his son.

Dream and dream big.

This chance encounter changed the course of my life—and, eventually, all my patients' lives—and forever redirected my Why. That hour's mentorship proved more valuable than any guidance I'd received in my previous twenty-nine years.

You see, ever since I was around nine years old, I've wanted to be a physician. I took the necessary prep courses in high school (even when everyone around me told me I couldn't) and enrolled as a pre-med student at the beginning of college. Taking these actions was an easy decision; I knew what I wanted to do.

Where, though, did that idea come from?

I'm not sure. Perhaps seeing my mother suffer after a traumatic car crash. Or maybe it was monitoring the cancer and surgery—a complete thyroidectomy—that caused her to take medications for the rest of her life. Perhaps it was my grandmother's debilitating polio, my father's lung cancer, my aunt's multiple sclerosis, or my grandfather's hepatitis. Without being able to put my finger on the exact root of the desire, I knew I wanted to take care of people in some sort of medical capacity.

With a few insightful questions and sixty minutes, Jim

reawakened that passion. After our talk, he gave me more than twenty books on tape that addressed personal growth and leadership; within days, I'd purchased a home study program for the Medical College Admission Test (MCAT). A few months later, I took the test (it didn't go as planned). While I wasn't admitted into the military's medical school, a few others looked at my application. Even though I, at thirty years old, was a nontraditional applicant, some schools offered me a chance. And while I was already on active duty, the Navy did not initially accept me into their scholarship program. However, a little prodding from my commanding officer persuaded the scholarship board to give me a second chance. I cannot thank him enough!

My life was headed in a new direction. Danika was pregnant; we were expecting our first child and life was drastically changing. I was shifting priorities and each day, my purpose became clearer and more established. No easy road lay ahead. The Process, I knew, was complex and I worried about failing. But I knew I had to stay the course.

END-OF-CHAPTER ASSESSMENT

Maybe several things provide your spark, but I want you to focus on one. This can be quite challenging, especially for super motivated people; focusing on only *one thing* may even seem ridiculous. A lot of power is generated by being mindful of that one thing. Remember: you are not required to go at it alone. A mentor can be a huge help in finding your Why. Just as we exist to help others with their problems, mentors do the same for us. These powerful motivators, influencers, and sounding boards can be instrumental in development and are available all around us, often waiting to be asked to help.

Questions for Reflection and Direction

Before moving on to the next chapter, take a moment to answer the questions in the space provided or in your journal. When you're ready, I'll meet you in Chapter 4.

THE PROCESS CHECKLIST

Priority 3: Your One Thing

1. What is that one thing that you think about every day?

_____

_____

_____

2. What is it about that one thing that keeps you coming back for more?

_____

_____

_____

3. Can you name three people you could look to and lean on for help in bringing your *one thing* to life?

_____

_____

_____

4. What traits make these three people best able to help you accomplish your goals and vision?

_____

_____

_____

5. Talk to each of these people listed; ask each for help uncovering your *one thing*. What did they say? Write what they tell you here and reflect on it daily.

_____

_____

_____

4 KNOWING WHO SITS AT YOUR TABLE

"Things which matter most must never be at the mercy of things which matter least."
—Johann Wolfgang von Goethe

GATHERING WHERE LIFE HAPPENS

I'd like to start this chapter by asking a question: "Who sits at your daily Table?"

You probably haven't been asked that before. I hadn't, until one of my friends posed a similar question during a talk on the value of life, and it got me thinking. Who do we spend our time with and what do we hope to achieve in our lives? The ideas that reflection spawned caused me to change the title of this chapter several times. I wanted to catch you off guard, grab your attention, and not let go.

What do I mean by "your Table"? The Table can be a physical structure, the place where you gather with friends and family to share a meal. It's also a metaphor: the Table is your life's nucleus. Let's explore what that could look like. For example, my Table includes Danika, Elle, and Siena, my wife and children. Is your Table populated with similar people or vastly different guests? Maybe you live with your mother, father, or another family member or friend. Perhaps you are the home's primary caretaker. Or maybe you sit alone at your Table. That's okay, too. There's no right or wrong answer. This is not a "right way or the highway" discussion. We're using the Table concept to determine who should be your high priority.

Your Table is where life happens—the Table becomes the experience. When you've fully analyzed and applied your priorities, relationships are more than superficial. Joy becomes the goal and odds of living a fulfilling life are high.

At that Table, stories are shared; decisions are made; lessons are taught. Round or square, wood or metal, real or imagined, a physical object isn't important. What matters are the souls gathered there. The Table is a communal place for life's love and fellowship, truth and candidness, and affirmation and justice. Within this circle is an opportunity for endless growth. You need to care for this gathering as you would a priceless piece of furniture. Keep it clean. Polish often; repair as needed. And always protect your Table; don't allow deep scratches or dings that cannot be repaired or buffed away to harm it.

As we dive more into this concept, I'd like to share something I recently heard while watching a movie. Numerous people (including my wife and children) enthusiastically recommended *The Greatest Showman*: "This film is great!" Right—I cynically figured my family just wanted me to buy the DVD. But from its enchanting entertainment to deeper life lessons, *The Greatest Showman* was truly a blessing, especially for anyone seeking personal growth. Others agree; I've read online reviews and even found a blog article titled "11 Financial Lessons from *The Greatest Showman*." On many levels, it looks like the producers, director, and screenwriter hit this one out of the park.

The musical is about P. T. Barnum, an American promoter who lived in the late 1800s and founded an iconic circus show. But the truth is *The Greatest Showman* is much more than an entertaining biopic. Its main message is that life is too short to spend doing something you don't love; life's relationships are what truly matter. In the film, Mr. Barnum hits rock bottom and loses his material possessions only to realize that certain intangible things are what bring true happiness.

The song "From Now On" expresses the pain Mr. Barnum experiences through his choices. He lives a true rags-to-riches story and climbs the American social ladder to dizzying heights. But tragedy strikes, and he realizes the special relationships he has built are fading. The resulting fall from public favor shattered his ego; Mr. Barnum, blinded by material wealth, had lost his purpose. That same disgrace, however, showed him a better definition of wealth—nothing mattered more than being surrounded by work he loved and people to share it with. Status and attention, favor from strangers who never really understood him or his passion, pale in comparison to love and those things that matter most in life.

You, too, can grasp what matters most in life. Like P. T. Barnum, you will then be able to endure many of the obstacles that come your way. If we set our Table appropriately and foster its surrounding relationships carefully, joy and happiness will fill our lives until the very end. Happiness doesn't come from fame and fortune. We must take care of what matters most—and the Table is one piece of that foundation.

ALONE AT THE TABLE

Some of you might be flying solo right now, and that is not a problem. It's okay to be the only one seated at your Table.

If you're by yourself, I urge you to try to develop peace and serenity with your Table. Find a way to appreciate your situation, whatever it is. Being solo might be something you've struggled with for some time. Maybe it's simply a season in your life. Right now, I'm in a season where my Table is full. As I experience raising two children, especially young ones who need their parents for everything, I look longingly at quiet moments; alone time doesn't come very often and when it does, I cherish it. While I love my girls more than anything, a little bit of quiet time is a gift.

Tables for one exist all around us. To paraphrase Emerson, we are the only ones who can grant ourselves peace. Have you ever been the first to arrive at a restaurant? Have you sat there, waiting for a friend? Instead of focusing on and lamenting the emptiness, think about whose company you'd treasure. Visualize the people you'd like to gather and, before very long, those empty seats will be filled and friends will line up, waiting their turn. You may even find you want and need a bigger Table!

The key to setting your Table is positive thinking. Own your current situation without complaint. Lamenting is for the lazy. Anyone reading this book who wants to improve their situation isn't lazy. So, stay focused on the positive. I've spent plenty of time on my own, without company, at my Table. For months, my truck's dashboard was where I broke bread, alone, and I was thankful for my situation. In fact, I've been thankful for that opportunity ever since.

Today, my Table is very different. I'm living in a different season, one where I work to provide for my family. That time alone, however, was crucial in preparing me for today's Table. Being alone, while hardly a requirement for success, can teach a tremendous amount about gratitude and finding good in any situation.

TURNING TRAGEDY INTO TRIUMPH

I'd like to share a story about a young man who, though broken at times, became an inspiration. Once you hear about his life, I think he'll be an inspiration to you, too. Jake Ashton exemplifies what it means to sit at your Table and how important perseverance is to pushing forward in life.

I first met Jake at a Golden Bears team dinner right before a road game against the University of Washington. I was on a four-week assignment from the Navy and handing out per diem money (ten years earlier, following my Process had led to volunteering with the team as a faculty fellow and volunteer assistant coach, and adhering to my priorities meant maintaining those friendships I'd built then). While handing out money wasn't part of my job, I volunteered to do it because I found meeting and connecting with every player on the team enlightening.

At this dinner, I handed each player his envelope. Inside was a daily allowance, some spending money to cover a snack or two during the weekend trip. Somehow Jake dropped his envelope in the team dining room. He looked for me right away to see if I had actually given it to him. I had given it to him, but somehow that hand-off turned into a fumble and he lost it. I had no choice but to help him find it. Minutes later, one of the staff members discovered the envelope (and Jake was elated, as thirty dollars can go a long way for a college athlete). In those few minutes of searching, however, we'd made a connection.

A few weeks later, before our game against the University of Arizona, I wrote Jake a letter—something personal, about finding his story inspiring, how he already possessed life's necessary skills, and that success on the field was his to achieve—and taped it to his locker. Even though he was getting ready for the game, he immediately sent me a text: "Jason, thank you so much for the letter. It caused me to shed a few tears." What a beautifully simple message. I had no idea my words would move him the way they did.

A week later, we were on the road to play the University of Colorado, and it was a calm night in the team hotel. Jake and I met to talk; for an hour, I listened to Jake's story. What I'd already heard from some of the coaches paled in comparison to the information Jake shared that night. He spoke with unexpected grace and elegance, and I was impressed by his conviction and dignity. There was little pride to get in the way, and Jake made it clear from the very beginning that he wanted no sympathy for his story, whatsoever. After we talked, I knew that, whether he believed it or not, the Process was something Jake believed in completely.

I had heard that Jake's parents died when he was young and he'd been shuttled from house to house and relative to relative. That's a short, unfeeling summary for a life—Jake fleshed out the details.

Jake's mother and father met while they were patients in a drug rehabilitation program. Everyone present and those family members awaiting their return agreed from the first moments: this was a relationship destined to fail. Their short courtship produced a child—Jake—and when his mother decide to move on, she left the baby behind. Jake's father had never finished school, though he'd attended the University of Southern California; lack of a college degree affected his psyche and ability to land a well-paying job. And then there was his addiction.

Time and time again, Jake's father relapsed. He also suffered from chronic liver disease; while he was in and out of the hospital, Jake's grandmother and uncle who lived in the Coachella Valley stepped in to help. Eventually, Jake and his father moved out of the greater Los Angeles area to be closer to them.

Times were tough. At one point, they had no car; father and son rode bikes wherever they needed to go. Food was scarce. Regular school was not an option for Jake—taking care of Dad had become his top priority. No one told him to do it. He assumed this caregiver role because, from the time he was seven or eight years old, it was the only thing he knew to do. Jake's father became severely ill; within days, his grandmother was diagnosed with cancer. Both were admitted to the hospital at the same time. Soon after, his father transitioned to hospice and passed away. Jake's grandmother died a few days later.

Where did this leave Jake? For a very brief time, Jake's mother tried to reenter his life. Having never known her, this contact felt strange to the boy. However, not long after her reappearance, she died, too (he's not sure what caused his mother's death; a heart attack?). How much devastation can one child absorb? His Uncle Lee, who had never been married nor raised a child, stepped in to become the male figure in Jake's life. That lack of experience didn't matter, though, as he wanted to help his nephew. Uncle Lee sought legal guardianship; he was to become a constant and supportive figure as Jake matured.

Despite having all the cards of a dysfunctional childhood stacked against him, despite spending many days and nights alone at his Table, Jake graduated from high school in 2014. He had excellent grades and, on his own accord, applied to a handful of colleges and universities throughout California. Jake was accepted by UC Berkeley—no one made a special phone call on his behalf; he had no connections to the school; he was accepted on his own merit. An excellent athlete, Jake garnered some attention from the university's football team and was eventually offered a scholarship.

What a success story! There was every reason for this well-spoken, inspiring young man to have failed. Jake was certainly fortunate that Uncle Lee became his guardian, providing him with a more stable home and general guidance. But make no mistake: Jake made that life happen. No one else could persevere for him. It takes a special kid to turn tragedy into triumph. Jake strived to pursue his dreams. Without realizing it, he worked the Process to his advantage.

THE CORE AND THE HEART

Picture a tall redwood tree, one with a thick trunk, massive branches, and roots so large you cannot simply step over them. I use this image as a metaphor for what I refer to as "the Core and the Heart," a way to explain the importance of those closest to us.

Let's take a deeper look at that beautiful redwood. Its thick tree trunk is fed and supported by those impressive roots. And the spreading network of branches projecting from the trunk span over and shelter everything below.

That redwood embodies the central relationships we have in life—our Core and Heart. These are the strongest relationships, the ones involving people you've chosen to join your daily Table.

Just like that redwood, our Core and Heart need daily care. We must draw nutrients into our central relationships and tend their various parts. Like a tree in nature, individuals grow together to form a strong, healthy, and absolute whole. Without roots, a sturdy trunk, and healthy branches, that redwood withers and dies. Our Core and Heart—those central relationships—are what allows us humans to function properly.

With this image in mind, I would contend that those closest to you help determine your journey through life. Now, while a tree cannot physically move, its "journey" consists of growth, and when not properly nourished, that redwood will weaken and eventually fall. When you're plagued by bad relationships, you won't get far, either. We need a strong Core and Heart to thrive. Tending our Table by carefully selecting, exercising, and feeding our central relationships keeps us nourished for life's journey. If we hope to go somewhere special in life, we must consider who is along for the ride and be sure to invite the best, most supportive people possible to our Table.

NOT ALL MINUTES ARE EQUAL

Now that you've set this Table, here comes the tough part: deciding how you will spend time with your Core and Heart. That's personal, and people often don't have the necessary insight to make good decisions. It's easy to be thoughtless, to get caught up in day-to-day activities without much thought regarding life's precious minutes.

Though each span sixty seconds, not all minutes are equal. How so? I think the following illustrates the concept well. Imagine cooking in the kitchen with your loved ones. (Now, because my wife enjoys her space and is always telling me and the girls to get out of "her" kitchen, this isn't easy for me. But deep down, I think Danika likes having us there—despite me getting in her way and the girls yelling, crying, cartwheeling, and making a mess.)

In your mind, do you see moments in the kitchen when everyone is smiling? Even when eggs are cracked and spilled on the floor, the bowl of mixed ingredients dumped, and someone fails to hear the oven timer go off, there can be happiness. After all, that togetherness in the kitchen is family time, an experience you'll likely cherish when things get tough and obstacles arise.

The minutes together in that kitchen are different from those spent at a restaurant or watching a game. They're part of the 86,400 seconds that comprise each day—and we get to decide how to use them.

Don't get me wrong. I'm not telling you to cancel plans with friends or that dinner reservation. I'm not advocating you eat every meal at home or turn off the television when the big game is on. That stuff is great; in fact, it's crucial. Those moments are part of human relationships, what separates us from the rest of the animal kingdom and every other living being on our planet. What I'm saying is that our minutes on this earth are equal to how we use them; therefore, we must diligently pursue what matters most to ensure we use our time wisely.

END-OF-CHAPTER ASSESSMENT

Throughout this chapter, we've discussed and learned about having your own Table, who sits at it, and how you tend to those relationships. Like me and millions of other people around the globe, you may find you're all by yourself at various points in life. Having no one else at your Table doesn't mean you're a bad person or a failure. Sometimes, being alone is beneficial; that space allows you to foster your ability for growth. Are there people at your Table? Congratulations! You must realize the value each of you offers the other. What lies at the Core and Heart is so very important when navigating choices about the time you've been given each day.

Questions for Reflection and Direction

Before moving on to the next chapter, take a moment to answer the following questions, either in the space provided or your journal. When you're ready, I'll meet you in Chapter 5.

THE PROCESS CHECKLIST

Priority 4: Your Daily Table

1. Fill in the names of people who sit at your Table.

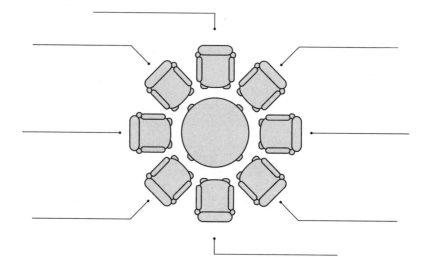

2. What can you do right now to improve your Table?

_____

_____

_____

3. What is usually discussed at your Table?

_____

_____

_____

4. Are you happy with discussions at your Table? If not, what would you rather be talking about?

_____

_____

_____

5. How are you enlivening and strengthening your Table today?

_____

_____

_____

5 BALANCING WORK AND PASSION

"The only way to do great work is to love what you do."
—Steve Jobs

BASICS AND NECESSITIES FIRST

Balancing our work and passion seems to be one of life's great trials. Work is that thing we do to provide for necessities; our passion is the thing we love to do, even if it doesn't provide for our basic needs. There are many reasons why we disregard our passions: we're tired after work, we don't have time, or we lose sight of their value in life when they don't put food on the table or clothes on our back.

For a select and fortunate few, work and passion are truly blended as one. In an ideal world, these would always blend into one homogeneous entity, with no barriers or borders to distinguish work from passion. But the reality is American society is not built that way, and most of us must experience the two separately.

When our work turns into passion, however, happiness grows.

A happy person is better able to deal with adversity and overcome fears. Happiness means our priorities are better aligned, and, as a result, life seems so much easier to manage.

Perhaps merging work and your passion into one and the same is not ideal for your situation. We're all different, and what succeeds for one doesn't necessarily bring joy for another. For me, the work-passion fusion makes everything else in life seem so much more valuable and worthwhile. But I understand how others contend these two endeavors should remain separate.

Earning a living, paying the bills, punching a clock—however you want to label work, its defining characteristic involves taking care of basics. Before you can think about saving and investing for your future or buying that car or home, there are things to spend on that you and your dependents need. Clean water to drink, food to eat, shelter, and clothing must be a priority. And it's usually a paycheck, not passion, that provides these things.

DELAYING GRATIFICATION

We should all strive to align work and passion as best we can. In simple terms, that alignment means doing what we want to do when we want to do it. We cannot all be professional golfers, Broadway actors, or CEOs of multimillion-dollar companies. Frankly, not everyone desires those things anyway. But each of us is very capable of discovering the silver lining that extends multiple passions into our work life.

An important key: this isn't going to happen overnight. And that's okay.

Aligning work and passion becomes a story of delayed gratification, and, unfortunately, that's not something most people enjoy practicing. Patience is difficult. It's not society's fault; humans are simply not wired for waiting. Our genetics and the survival of the fittest paradigm fight postponing gratification. But if we can practice patience and wait, our long-term goals become achievable.

Let's start with money. Perhaps your background is like mine: I was lucky to get a pat on the back when I completed high school or left home the first time. Maybe you, too, lived in your car and had nothing. Or perhaps you started off on a better financial foot, with a wealthy family and an inherited fortune. We all come from different circumstances and all are dealt different cards. But to get ahead, to save and see finances grow, you must start with money. It's important to have funds to invest in the future, so we can do more of the things we want to do when we want to do them.

Everyone's management strategies will be different, and I'm not here to instruct you on finances—I'm simply pointing how successfully managing your money leads to a life well lived. A few basic tips (and these following items are indeed very basic) will easily help improve your financial situation dramatically.

LIVING WITHIN YOUR MEANS

Perhaps you've heard the expression "keeping up with the Joneses." These fictional neighbors are always one step ahead of us. When the Joneses buy a shiny new SUV, your older sedan feels cramped. The Joneses' kids have all the latest tech gadgets. Consequently, when you don't buy the same gizmos (and your kids aren't afraid to let you know when this happens), you feel like a lousy parent. Besides the feelings of inadequacy that keeping up with the Joneses instills, the biggest problem with comparing ourselves to others is losing sight of one simple fact: we're not *supposed* to be the same. Each of us, with our individual priorities and unique family situations, is on our own different unique life journey.

Trying to keep up with the Joneses, Kardashians, or whoever else you think has it better than you, can wreak havoc on your finances.

Wealthy people go broke chasing those same insecurities, as hard as that may be to believe. Instead of more stuff, we need more balance. We should live within our means, without overindulging by spending too much . . . and without depriving ourselves of simple pleasures by spending too little.

This sense of financial balance was ingrained in me at a young age by my immigrant parents. My father, who arrived from the Azores Islands with nothing more than a passport, a few dollars, and a set of clothes, lacked a formal education but he learned on life's battlefield. He never worried about keeping up with the Joneses; Dad had no clue who the Joneses were. Chasing the American Dream was not his Process—he was searching for freedom. With steadfast discipline, he used keen business sense and basic skills and tools—cutting and hauling firewood with a chainsaw and a truck—to provide shelter, food, and, most importantly, a sense of pride for his family.

But Dad never took it to the next level; he settled with basic comforts. Is that because selling firewood was not demanding (although the physical aspect was anything but easy)? Or was it because my father lacked the education and business acumen to turn his ideas into something more? I'll never know for sure. Any big-time CEO would have seen Dad's lack of business growth as a failure. To be blatantly honest, I always wondered why he didn't do more; that others considered my family lower class always embarrassed me.

Now, as I look back on my childhood, I am quite thankful. Material items would've been nice to have, but money never got in my way of being able to think. I never had the luxury of adopting an "I need it now" mentality. So, from an early age, I developed a balanced perspective about finances. I saw that the amount of money my parents earned was equal to what they paid for the goods we needed to survive. We didn't have credit cards, we didn't owe anyone anything, and we didn't live above our means. But that meant my folks were unable to save for when hard times were truly hard, so I quickly realized this delicate balance kept us from getting ahead.

Is keeping up with the Joneses causing your life to swing out of balance? If so, take a couple of steps back. Review your financial situation. Adjust to spend on those basics and requirements you need and, eventually, the economic scales will even themselves out. And before you know it, you'll have the means for those jaw-dropping pursuits—life's real adventures, not the ones only seen on TV.

MONEY, MONEY, MONEY

Whether you grew up rich or poor, money is a driving force in our lives. What makes the difference for most of us are the role models we had while we were growing up. That bad history or math teacher can easily be forgotten and made up for the next school year. But when you live and grow up under the guidance and example of someone who just doesn't get financial responsibility, chances are you will struggle economically your entire life. That is, until you learn to break free from their Process.

How a family handles money has a lasting and profound effect, just like the chromosomes and DNA we harbor. Think of that behavior as imprinted—and running away from our personal blueprint is hard work that requires dedication. What you accomplish in the financial arena—income, debt, spending, and saving—will be a part of your legacy.

MONEY MANAGEMENT PRINCIPLES

Here are some simple money management principles that I live by. These principles have saved me lots of time—time I didn't lose to stressing out about paying off debt. They are as follows:

1. Don't spend more than you make.

2. Build an emergency fund that equals at least six months of your salary (it may take some time to get there, and that's okay).

3. Prioritize spending. Food, clothing, and shelter should be top of the list.

4. Start a retirement account. Even if you can only put in twenty-five or fifty dollars each month, that savings is about compounding interest—which builds a much greater savings over the long run.

5. Put an affordable percentage of your earnings into a savings account or retirement fund each month. This ensures you are setting some money aside for yourself before addressing basic expenses.

You probably already use many of these financial principles; perhaps you have your own methods, but this is an area in life that, if mismanaged, can easily create life-long repercussions. Managing finances is all part of The Process, and neglecting this piece has resulted in many a divorce and bankruptcy. Taking a little extra time now to learn a little more about finances—in general and your own—will save you time and money (and heartache) later. Start by drawing out a monthly budget. Running into setbacks that could've been prevented by a few extra seconds spent on financial planning is frustrating. Concentrate on the big picture—money for the future—instead of grabbing the instant gratification in quick spending here and now.

IN PRAISE OF PATIENCE

Delayed gratification. I don't know what it is, but this concept really inspires me. Whenever I hear a story about waiting to celebrate, I get excited. Perhaps my sentiments are related to all the lessons gained from putting pleasure off until later. There's something special about waiting (even if you wait too long and miss what it is you're waiting for). Perhaps my personal experience has primed me to accept delayed gratification.

Navy SEALs and other elite military personnel harness the power of delayed gratification better than most. These warriors can see past obstacles on their way to successfully completing any given mission. This belief blooms with the first day of training; a class of Navy SEAL recruits starts with 150 to 180 eager, able bodies. That number, however, begins to dwindle within a few hours. Only those with the mental and physical toughness will make it to the final day of SEAL training. Not everyone can see past pain and exhaustion to the reward at the end of training, and those who lack that ability will ring the bell, asking to be removed from the training.

But you don't need to be an aspiring Navy SEAL to understand, or even believe in, the power of delayed gratification. All you need to do is focus on what The Process can do for you.

The challenge is that we live in an "instant" world. Many people take on jobs and careers because they do not see the value in waiting, or at least pausing and taking a few breaths, to figure out what truly inspires them. That inspiration is what transforms a life. Passion unlocks your internal motivation and propels you to places you've only dreamed about, where limits are for those who *choose* to set them. When you are passionate about something, if you care enough to dream it (and, more importantly, then do it), you're not just working.

A serving of delayed gratification can give you the time to become inspired. I invite you to take care of the necessities we previously discussed and then focus on your passions. Use your new appreciation of delay as fuel to achieve your desires, and don't allow anything to hold you back. Accept the benefits that employment brings; enjoy the work you are passionate about. Delay your celebration just a little bit and, before you know it, you'll be on the path toward turning work and passion into one big reward.

COMBINING WORK AND PASSION

We've covered the necessities, examined the simple area of saving, and discussed how your money grows through the power of compounding. Now let's return to the idea of combining work and passion.

A survival mentality—living day to day and paycheck to paycheck—increases stress and keeps you from fulfilling your dreams. Or extends the time necessary to make them a reality. You have to plan for the future to realize your dreams, and persistence is a major factor in thinking ahead.

Persistence keeps you in the game and sets you back on course if you become derailed. Persistence changes cultures. And when you are persistent in pursing what you truly feel passionate about, nothing can stop you. Nothing, that is, but *you.*

How do you know if you are really following your passion? A lot of things, after all, may be exciting and interesting. While defining passion may be a little different for each of us, I believe that a recurring theme is being so focused and authentically lost in your pursuit that two things happened: you lose track of time and are extremely comfortable with that loss. Because you love what you're doing, there is no anxiety over time spent. This total dedication is where you actually experience joy in your life. And when you fail in some aspect of doing what you love, the pain of failure doesn't sting quite so badly. You'll be relieved and content to get back up and keep going, since being immersed in the task, that passion, is exactly where you want to be.

WHEN WORK DOES NOT EQUAL PASSION

What about when your work fails to form a symbiotic relationship with passion? It's not pretty. Your journey through life gets bumpy, full of potholes, roadblocks, and dead-ends all around. You become worn out and bitter. Perhaps you accept that this is how life is and never try for more. Too many people give up, and this lack of trying stems from failing to align priorities. Just because there's no passion in our work doesn't mean that we can't achieve it later.

My journey has had many diversions, not all of them ideal or scenic. But I'm certain that these detours from life's route are all a necessary part of The Process. From living in my pickup truck to joining the Navy, from flying planes to my current role of helping people overcome ailments and find more meaningful lives, I've been consistently closing the gap on combining work with passion.

You, too, must continue to follow your passion. If you don't, you won't fully enjoy your life, and I don't think there's anything sadder than not having the self-worth to give yourself a fighting chance. If you give up on finding a way to align work with passion, I see bad things ahead: moving from job to job without fulfillment; having your home life fall apart; becoming disillusioned and entering a dark alley of despair. Avoiding the bad involves choosing to try.

When I look back, the moment in my life that most stands out involves decision-making—when I chose to join the Navy and fly airplanes. I was in my third year of college, fully engaged in a pre-medical program, when my roommate and I attended a career fair. The materials we'd picked up included information about the military. Joining seemed like a very good idea. Medical school was going to cost hundreds of thousands of dollars and my odds of getting in were quite low. Serving in the military would be an honorable and selfless profession, one that could help me pay for medical school.

There was even an option of becoming a military physician, which would cover medical school expenses, guarantee a job, and provide a lifetime of worldwide adventures after I completed training. Without a mentor to advise me differently, that was it; I was sold. Within just a few days, I'd begun the process by completing and submitting the application. I passed the physical exam and months later, I'd enlisted in the United States Navy.

My father and I hadn't spoken for more than four years but had we talked, I know he'd have advised against my enlistment. He had good reason for his feelings; drafted into the Portuguese military at age seventeen, he'd served as a Green Beret, on the frontlines in treacherous conflicts in Africa during the 1960s and 1970s. Some of the African leaders practiced perverse guerrilla warfare, heinous dictators who cared only about supreme power. How my father survived more than five years in such circumstance is beyond me. In the military I'd serve in, multimillion-dollar aircraft, weapons of mass destruction, and computer systems could destroy an enemy from thousands of miles away, and six- to twelve-month deployments got complaints. My father and his brothers-in-arms lived, fought, and survived in a completely different world.

When I enlisted, I hardly knew what that service entailed. For the first ten years, though the Iraqi and Afghanistan conflicts were in full gear, work often felt like nothing more than putting on a uniform. I was flying in various aircraft, going on great adventures, and seeing the world from sea level and thirty thousand feet or more in the sky. At times my colleagues and I would agree that we were "at the tip of the sphere." I had the opportunity to further my education and became an adjunct professor and student advisor, joining the ranks at one of best public universities in the world. Truly, I couldn't complain. Life was great. Yet I felt empty inside.

The fun I was having didn't move me the way I needed to be moved. Teaching at UC Berkeley was awesome. Mentoring the midshipmen was even better. The coaching assignment with the football team was great. What a life! But deep down, I recognized I was not completely passionate about all of it. I wanted something more, and my persistent childhood dream about becoming a physician reappeared.

Medical school and residency training, with many weeks working eighty-plus hours at a stretch, taught me that when you are truly passionate about something, you can weather the tough times. Passion makes everything—including work—a lot easier to handle, and those eight years are a testament to that. I am now closer than ever to fusing work and my passion. And you can experience this joy, too.

Perhaps it's time to reflect about where your passions lie. Think without judging; don't repress what has happened but accept your life's trajectory. Appreciate the journey you are on and keep looking for ways to make living your passion a real possibility.

END-OF-CHAPTER ASSESSMENT

I hope you've gained some appreciation for the greatness that may develop when work and passion combine. Taking care of the necessities, learning how to save (and make those savings grow), and being mindful of patience (hello, delayed gratification!) can help achieve your dreams. The goal for any of us with a zest for life? Doing what we love and getting paid for it. Dreams get placed on hold when we quit trying, when we fail to choose happiness. But that work-passion fusion can happen—we might not exactly know when or how we might get there, and that's okay. The journey and discovery are all part of The Process.

Questions for Reflection and Direction

Before moving on to the next chapter, take a moment to answer the questions below, either in the space provided or your journal. When you're ready, I'll meet you in Chapter 6.

THE PROCESS CHECKLIST

Priority 5: Your Work and Passion

1. Is your work fulfilling? If so, how? If not, why not?

_____

_____

_____

2. List three things about your current work that could help you live your passion.

_____

_____

_____

3. What's one thing you could do to fuse work and passion?

_____

_____

_____

4. How are you saving and preparing for your future?

_____

_____

_____

5. What can you do to keep your passion burning tomorrow?

_____

_____

_____

6 MAKING TIME FOR FAMILY AND FRIENDS

"The quality of our relationships is what determines the quality of our lives."

—Esther Perel

MISERY LOVES COMPANY

Remember when I brought up the concept of your Table? How you set it and decide who to include? If you completed the exercise at the end of Chapter 4, you filled in the Table graphic with names (and those seats may or may not have all been occupied). Now, we're going to go one step further and extend the Table concept to include those you don't nest with—people you care deeply about but may not interact with on a routine basis. Let's face it: life is complex. Work, hobbies, adversities, dreams—all these get in the way of time with our Core and Heart. The question becomes, who do you invite to your Table? And, once invited, who stays? Who returns often, and which people must be turned away?

This is where we face the realities of being human and become comfortable with our choices. It's not that you should never invite certain people to your Table; creating boundaries, saying no—even though we want to please everyone—can be hard and nearly impossible. But if we want others to value us, they must observe that we value ourselves first. When we stand up for ourselves, those close to us are witnesses, especially when we are saying no to them.

Let's take a deeper look at things that might get in the way of our Process. Even a perfect checklist with set priorities cannot give us the desired time to do everything we want to achieve day after day.

Have you heard the phrase "misery loves company"? I'm guessing you have but just in case, here's an example about dating to paint this picture.

Let's say you're a young woman with a long-time friend, a girl you've known for many years. Six months ago, the two of you went out with a group for an evening of dinner and dancing. While on the town, you met another party of people enjoying the same activities; everyone exchanged stories and shared dance moves, phone numbers, and Twitter handles. Two of those connections blossomed into romance and within weeks, you and your friend had established new relationships. It was as if you'd won the lottery or Olympic gold and taken a dream trip to a faraway destination! Fun days and nights with these love interests happily consumed your waking hours.

But then, the new boyfriend stopped calling your pal. He suddenly disappeared altogether, even un-friending her on Facebook. Distraught and miserable, your friend was barely able to function; she clearly needed you. So, you were there. You listened. You cried with and consoled her. You did everything you knew how to comfort her. You even cooled it with your new beau, saying you needed a couple of days for your friend.

Two days turns into four and then you realize two weeks have passed without seeing your new love. While getting ready one morning, brushing your teeth and putting on makeup, you take a deep look in the mirror and see dark circles under your eyes. Pimples dot your chin and forehead; your skin looks terrible; you're exhausted and sad. How did this happen? Breaking into tears, you realize your friend's misery has found its company in *you*.

That sudden realization causes your focus to shift: you've gone from wanting to help and support your friend to hating and resenting her demands. How could she take advantage of you? But it hits you—she isn't the only one to blame for your anger and sadness.

*   *   *

Can you relate to this story? It doesn't have to be about dating; it could be about anything—losing a job, death of a loved one, not winning that award, missing out on an end-of-the-year bonus, or something quite minor. Misery comes in all shapes and forms. Think of it like being lactose intolerant and faced with Baskin-Robbins' thirty-one flavors. A friend offers you a cone and you're enticed to take a few licks; oh, it tastes so good! Before you know it, you've eaten an entire scoop. Then, the lactose sets in and your stomach starts cramping. Eventually, your self-image deteriorates ("How could I be so weak? I know I can't eat ice cream!"). You may even punish yourself with time at the gym to "exercise it off" and berate yourself for weight gain.

This, my friends, is misery. Regardless of the source, such bad feelings are hard to combat unless your priorities and The Process are in place.

SETTING YOUR EXTENDED TABLE

In my search for people with great stories full of adversity, growth, and "come to Jesus" moments, I landed upon Terry Crews. Mr. Crews is an actor, former professional football player, artist, husband, and father. While I was familiar with Mr. Crews from his movies, it wasn't until an interview on the Tim Ferriss Show that I learned his heart and soul. He was funny and had a magnetizing personality. I won't recap the entire podcast here (it's easy to find; in fact, I encourage you to listen to Mr. Crews tell his own story). But I would be remiss if I didn't include a summary, because his life is one of mastering priorities and living through The Process.

Something Mr. Crews discussed really resonated with me—the topic was letting people go. He paints a beautiful landscape of relationships with his words. "Relationships do not have to end bad," Mr. Crews said, "but they often have to end when things are not right." He gave an example of a friendship that had become toxic: "We just cannot hang out anymore."

You see, Mr. Crews was setting his Table. He understands that we should never let anyone define who we are. He understands the importance of monitoring who sits at your Table. He gets that developing one's sense of self is key to a healthy Table. It's that simple. Those core relationships—our Table—are a priority for each of us, something we should all value and make our very own.

As you've come to realize from reading *Exceptional Every Day*, relationships are the underlying theme of our priorities and the heart of The Process.

Relationships are ubiquitous; we have a relationship with ourselves, our friends and family members, coworkers, and casual acquaintances (baristas, hair dressers, physicians, and yoga instructors). Like Mr. Crews, I've had a few toxic relationships throughout my life, and, unfortunately, I didn't end them soon enough. You've probably had one or two yourself—or perhaps you're tangled in one right now. None of us are immune (how many books with "toxic" and "relationship" in their titles have been written?), so I invite you to read this section carefully.

Take some time to carefully consider who sits at your Table and ask yourself, does he or she *deserve* to be there?

This is *your* life. All you need to do is be true to yourself. If someone wants to be at your Table, the only choice is whether you want him or her there. If your experience with that person is positive, go for it. If not, move on. You owe it to yourself.

DEALING WITH TOUGH SITUATIONS

News flash: you cannot micro-manage others or time spent with them.

For the majority of us, being honest with friends and family is difficult. We would like to follow the Golden Rule and avoid hurting anyone's feelings. This can be especially difficult when managing time with others. Though we love them, people may say or do things that go completely against our grain. And yet there we are, stuck together at the Table.

I am reminded of American businessman Jack Welch, who once said, "Control your own destiny or someone else will." My wife and I had to implement this strategy not that long ago when Danika received a highly insulting voicemail. I was using her phone (it was my first attempt at acupuncture and I wanted a photo of her back so we'd remember this day, in case I totally botched the treatment) when I noticed she had a voicemail. I pointed it out and we played the recording. The first thirty seconds or so were full of static, rumblings, and random words; clearly, the recording was accidental. Out of curiosity, we continued listening. Boom! We recognized the voices; her parents were ranting about none other than yours truly!

I won't bore you with the details, but they exchanged some

choice words about how I lived life (you know, conservative with money, driving an old truck, serving in the military). Something you should know about my in-laws: in their eyes, the only people who can do no wrong are a select few of their children. Four kids between them plus five from other relationships is a grand total of nine—and only three out of the bunch are "perfect." Would you believe they have many grandchildren they've never met?

Our family (Danika, our children, and I) has had no communication with my wife's parents for nearly seven years. Why? It's a sad and painful explanation. When our first daughter, Elle, was born, these people wouldn't hold her and faked illness to avoid coming to the hospital for a subsequent visit. My father-in-law uttered the worst words I'd ever heard; he referred to our precious child using the n-word.

Is it any wonder we stopped communicating? Thanks to the Navy, we left California for four years and, during that time, no one on either end kept in touch. That lack of contact was liberating. My wife's father—who describes himself as a self-made man and multimillionaire—grew up in Boyle Heights, a rough neighborhood in East Los Angeles, and was kicked out of many schools. Eventually, he joined the Army; he got kicked out of that, too! Do I need to point out that this is a man with no clear sense of purpose or Why in his life? He once told me that, as a military man, I could never raise a family (I think I've proven him wrong on that). His actions at the hospital show how all the money in the world cannot provide a clear Process. If you squander relationships by constantly disrespecting others, thinking you are better, even disowning your own children, life will have very little meaning. In this case, The Process can only result in failure.

Still, I felt bad and thought we should try to pay my wife's parents a visit so they could meet our daughters. Danika was against the idea, but I thought it was important that she either receive closure (which she hadn't gotten when we moved away) or become the bigger person and move forward. A visit rather than a phone call seemed best.

Danika and I put our faith in The Process; we trusted that everything would work out as it should and we expected nothing great in return. Unfortunately, the judgment and disrespect picked right up where they'd left off. And this resulted in a valuable lesson—the experience confirmed that some people never change and, in the case of toxic relationships, we must accept facts and move on. Even though we haven't been in contact with my in-laws since that incident, Danika and I are better off for reaching out, sure that our life's choices are right for us and our children.

I hope this story resonates with you and that, thanks to my sharing this painful slice of extended family life, you're able to avoid similar situations. Knowing how I've handled this tough scenario can help you make better decisions when dealing with difficult family interactions. Remember: you can't control these negative people or manage that time with them. Avoiding the quagmire of toxic relationships throughout your journey will enable you to judge less and consider more carefully who should truly sit at your daily Table.

THE IMPORTANCE OF FRIENDSHIP

A good friend, someone who is truly there for the right reasons, is an uncommon occurrence. Take a moment to tally up how many close friends you have; I think the number will surprise you. I am fortunate to have a few of those friends. One of them is Todd Travers.

Todd's that friend who wants to help, even when I don't need it. When I do need a boost, he's the first to step up. Over the years of our friendship, I've grown to accept the fact that there's no shame in asking for help when you need it.

Together, Todd and I have taken apart the gas tank on Danika's car (an all-day affair). While a big part of that adventure had to do with saving money, the other part was spending time together, bonding, and enjoying the moment. Another time, we assembled a furnace for Todd's parents, a multiday affair full of twists and turns (all while Todd's father hovered); the experience was an "all minutes are not equal" event, where time spent—even if exhausting—has special, affirming meaning. Todd and I have completed many other projects together and, through it all, that guy quite simply wants to be my friend, no strings attached.

The self-proclaimed black sheep in his family (he's the only one who did not attend UC Berkeley), Todd often discredits how smart he is. Thanks to his profound work ethic and some wise investing, Todd's at a point where he sets his own schedule and donates as much personal time as he desires. That entails volunteering with the UC Berkeley football team. He loves the experiences gained— camaraderie, travel, and games—from being a part of the program. What Todd's looking for isn't recognition or compensation. Todd, a great person with a big heart and a kind spirit, understands The Process and just how valuable and important it is. While I don't get how he can watch mechanic and garage shop shows, listen to country music for hours on end, or be so overly demonstrative in his admiration for the military, I'm convinced Todd's passion to help and how he values relationships are things everyone can learn from. I share the story of our friendship so you have a worthy example in mind as you set your extended Table.

GETTING YOUR PRIORITIES IN ORDER

Once you've figure out your priorities, managing time for friends and family becomes a lot less stressful. So, let's talk about social media.

Previously unimagined and unknown technology has enabled ready communication and access on a global level. On one hand, this is amazing! But this technological advancement comes with a downside, especially one related to friendship and time management. Platforms like Instagram, Facebook, LinkedIn, and WhatsApp have allowed an unprecedented connection with people around the world. However, that easy access also creates a time-sucking vortex.

When I first joined the Navy, smartphones weren't that smart. Mail was truly snail mail (while I was on deployment once, Danika sent a care package—I saw her in Hong Kong before the package made it my way; when it did, the treats inside were old and stale). Email access was anything but accessible; once available, our correspondence was screened by some shipboard secret squirrel before it ever reached the world wide web. That's how it was back then. But things changed.

Over the next ten years, technology exploded and the Navy granted more liberal access to it. FaceTime and Skype allowed soldiers, sailors, and airmen on remote bases to remain connected with their families like never before; the morale-boosting ability to share photos, videos, text, and emotions within seconds was available for anyone with access to a computer, tablet, or smartphone. Staying connected was easy; dialing a number, changing out of your pajamas, brushing your teeth, or leaving home wasn't necessary. That convenience, however, is a big part of the trouble with this type of technology.

Do you know anyone who's so caught up with social media that they stay on for hours, skip meals and workouts, forget to pick up the kids, and neglect other daily tasks? Don't confuse this compulsion with passion; plugging in to social media is like being in a Las Vegas casino without a clock in sight.

The convenience of technology being at your fingertips at all hours of the day creates other problems, too. Scientific studies now prove many mood disorders can be attributed to social media use.[3]

---

3   Primrack et. al, Social Media Use and Perceived Social Isolation Among Young Adults in the U.S. *American Journal of Preventive Medicine*, Vol 53, Issue 1, https://www.ajpmonline.org/article/S0749-3797(17)30016-8/fulltext.

My own clinical experience involves many patients, mostly between the ages of fifteen and thirty-five, who suffer from anxiety, depression, and "adjustment disorders" (a newer medical term describing a group of symptoms—stress, sadness, hopelessness, and various physical symptoms—that can occur after stressful life events) resulting from their social media use.

Now, all social media use isn't bad. But what we want to remember is that it can interfere with The Process: learning about yourself; taking in amazing experiences; looking, listening, smelling, tasting, and feeling what abounds around you. No computer or technological advancement can ever replace actual experience. No screen image can ever replace the live person staring back. Don't miss out on the gift that The Process delivers; use social media as a tool, not a replacement for maintaining human connections.

WHO NEEDS YOU?

Deciding whom to spend our precious and fleeting seconds with might be one of the most difficult decisions we ever make. Therefore, it's important to know your priorities, have a plan, and implement your Process. The Process is your lifeblood—it feeds your ability to make decisions. And that will come in handy when challenges surface.

SEVEN INSIGHTS

I like to read. As I was writing, I was searching for some insight into daily struggles I'd observed and experienced at work, so I picked up *Growing Physician Leaders*, a book by retired Army Lieutenant General Mark Hertling. Using various viewpoints, *Growing Physician Leaders* illustrated some of the issues my colleagues and I were experiencing a sense of burnout and sort of unfulfilled purpose—and shed light on challenging situations, including how to support caregivers (folks tending to loved ones), address end-of-life care with patients, and look out for your coworkers. Lt. Gen. Hertling did not directly address these points, but what I read presented these issues in a different, more upfront way. At the end of the book, one of Lt. Gen. Hertling's students wrote about his experience in the general's physician leader course. That student was Dr. Christopher "Joe" Smith, chair of medicine at Florida Hospital, and he concluded with seven key insights important for any leader and every relationship.

Consider Dr. Smith's seven insights and then apply them to every relationship you choose to maintain or create. Can you see their value at your Table? These seven insights are, in fact, the glue that keeps your Table together:

1. Be on time.

2. Actively cooperate.

3. Humility invites kindness.

4. Optimism invites trust.

5. Trust is the gateway to opportunity.

6. Be concise.

7. Familiarity is superior to formality.

END-OF-CHAPTER ASSESSMENT

Now that you're roughly halfway through the book, your Process is becoming reality. In this chapter, you reviewed different types of relationships and how they affect our time. Whether these relationships feel like a daily added value or misery with each step, our lives are made more complex by the people we choose to include. Selecting who sits at your Table and when to spend time with them is critical. We must also avoid superficial connection through social media, how it connects and drains us, to effectively use the time and technology available. In the next section, I will challenge you to take inventory of your digital life and Table to create balance as you cultivate fruitful relationships.

Questions for Reflection and Direction

Before moving on to the next chapter, take a moment to answer the following questions, either in the space provided or your journal. When you're ready, I'll meet you in Chapter 7.

THE PROCESS CHECKLIST

Priority 6: Your Family and Friends

1. You've read the chapter; now, take inventory of your Table. Is it bigger? Smaller? Make any updates to your Table in the graphic below.

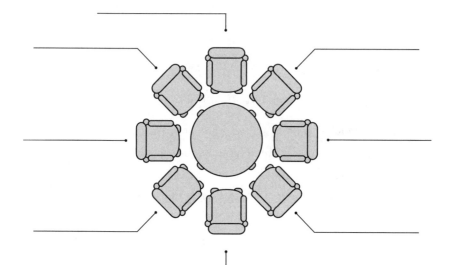

2. List all your digital devices in the space provided.

_____

_____

_____

3. Now, turn off all digital devices for at least two days. Keep a list of your emotions, activities, and accomplishments during this period; record them here.

_____

_____

_____

4. List any friends or family members whose misery brings you down.

_____

_____

_____

5. Now, create a break-away plan. Outline how you'll escape those downer friends and family and include ways to handle possible consequences in the space provided.

_____

_____

_____

7 PRIORITIZING MIND AND BODY

"To give anything less than your best is to sacrifice the gift."
—Steve Prefontaine

As we begin this next chapter, I'd like you to think about which components of your health and well-being matter the most. This is a tough question, one that might take a few minutes or more to answer. As a physician and personal growth coach, my goal is multifaceted, yet it reduces to one essential paradigm: I want to help people live better, healthier, and more productive lives.

Let's focus on *living better*. What, you may be wondering, do I mean by that phrase? I've broken my explanation into the following factors:

- Mental and physical abilities

- Comfort and serenity

- Enjoyable activities

- Relationships with others

- Possessions

THE IMPORTANCE OF EXERCISE

As we examine *living better*, I'd like to start with our bodies. And we can't talk about bodies without discussing physical abilities.

How many of you fit exercise into your week? This is an important question, one I ask often. Many of my colleagues and many more of my patients treat exercise as an afterthought or shove it to the bottom of the priority list. Why? I believe a big piece of the problem lies in our perception of exercise. One of the primary roadblocks is differing views about what constitutes exercise and how that relates to physical activity.

Many athletes would claim a thirty-minute brisk walk does not count as exercise. If you're not sweating aggressively, working out for hours on end, and raising that heart rate, you're not achieving healthful benefits. However, I could show you study after study validating walking, one of the best low-impact exercises, as a means of exercise. Whatever your unique limitations might be, walking is easily adaptable: in a swimming pool, indoors (at the gym or shopping center), stairwells. Whatever the space you have, walking works—you just need to be creative.

Exercise is essential for physical and mental health, and it doesn't have to be difficult or strenuous to be effective. It does, however, need to become a priority in your life. However you choose to exercise, it should be something that's easily accomplished and—just like showering, brushing your teeth, and eating—occupies a "can't miss" slot on your daily schedule. Somehow, we manage to complete other activities that keep us healthy and free from illness yet, once we feel too busy, the first thing we drop is exercise.

Perhaps putting off exercise is easier because its benefits are often not immediately seen. Even after weeks of regular exercise, weight remains stable (or even goes up) and our pants fit the same. Beneficial changes to our cardiovascular and respiratory systems may be invisible, and many of us are impatient (remember that concept of delayed gratification?). Those of us who get discouraged and quit are looking at exercise all wrong. The fault here lies in perception of benefits. Ultimately, exercise enhances, improves, and prolongs lives. When we exercise, cells regenerate, muscles repair faster, kidneys eliminate waste better, and hearts pump blood more efficiently. The invisible changes are the most important ones.

GETTING STARTED

Now that we've scratched the surface about the importance of regular exercise, let's explore how to incorporate exercise into our lives. Many of us put exercise in the backseat and move other obligations to the front. Often, it takes an adverse health event to propel many of us to reevaluate our priorities. And that wake-up call can come in many forms. Think about chest pain—whether associated with physical activity, stress, or emotional causes, you'll seek out medical attention and then address that problem, often by getting into shape. That reactive mindset, more often than not, comes too late.

Though medicine has come a long way, with new medications, procedures, and interventions popping up daily, not every health issue can be fixed. Change your thinking right now; instead of being reactive (waiting for that bad event to spark a change), get preventative by eliminating resistance to regular exercise. You may be surprised to discover how much better even one day of conscious decision-making surrounding your fitness and health can make you feel.

Exercise alone isn't the key to better health. We've got to talk about nutrition. Ditch the cigarettes or Twinkies, loosen the grip on that fountain drink, and opt for an edible protein at every meal (eggs at breakfast, for example, instead of a sugar-laden bowl of cereal). I didn't put this chapter at the beginning of the book, but this placement doesn't make it any less relevant or important. Health and fitness = life, and I'm about to show you just how easy this can be. So, grab some food storage containers so you can start planning and prepping your meals for the week ahead, fill up a bottle of plain H2O, open your notebook so you can write some of this stuff down, and let's get started. It's time you gave your mind and body what they deserve.

FIVE STARTING EXERCISES

Does "exercise" cause you a little apprehension? Perhaps you're picturing unpleasant activities, workouts you don't think you'd enjoy. As a result, you decide to do nothing. Unfortunately, this outlook on exercise is self-defeating and can detrimentally affect your overall health and well-being.

In late 2017, the Centers for Disease Control and Prevention (CDC) published a report stating a steady increase in American obesity. Data from 1999–2000 was compared with that from 2015–2016, which clearly demonstrated rates of obesity had increased from 30.5 to 39.6 percent among adults and from 13.9 to 18.5 percent in youth age 2 to 19 years old.[4] These numbers are abominable and truly heartbreaking. It's easy for someone like me who's involved in health and wellness to see how real this epidemic is, and I attribute blame to many factors.

More sedentary lifestyles, longer commutes, increased personal obligations, an explosion of processed foods in the American diet—huge cultural shifts contribute to this epidemic. However, we can all do our part to fight obesity. Start with exercise. If you don't already have an exercise plan, begin with five minutes of movement per day. Pick a regular time: right after you wake up, pull in the driveway from work, take a lunch break, or following dinner. You could

---

4   From "The State of Childhood Obesity," by Trust for America's Health and the Robert Wood Foundation, https://stateofobesity.org/childhood-obesity-trends/.

even exercise while watching television! Whatever you do can be simple—a stroll with family, brisk walk at work, easy stretches and flexing. Adding exercise to your day shouldn't be difficult. Give it a try. With all the great things exercise can do for you, I don't think you'll be disappointed.

To help you get moving, I wanted to share a few simple exercise ideas. These can be done even when you don't think you have the time. All can easily become part of your routine. Whether done daily or every other day, regular exercise will reap health benefits right away. Here are five suggestions for starting your new active routine:

1. Swimming
2. Tai chi
3. Strength training
4. Walking
5. Kegel exercises

Though not long, this list contains quite effective exercises for maintaining general fitness. Bonus: all can be adapted to meet specific needs and were chosen to give you the best shot at leading a functional, happy, and productive life. Here's a closer look at each of these exercises so you can evaluate their benefits and consider which to implement into your Process:

- **Swimming:** This low-impact exercise puts less stress on joints and is great for those with arthritis. As little as thirty to forty-five minutes a few times per week builds aerobic fitness, and studies have shown swimming elevates moods, battles depression, and decreases stress.

- **Tai chi:** Go to any park in a large city, and you'll see groups (often older Asian men and women) performing slow martial arts-type movements. Tai chi is graceful and flowing; the set practice is "moving meditation" that works on balance and coordination, which are especially important as we age. Another related exercise option: yoga, a close sibling of tai chi.

- **Strength training:** This includes many forms and types— bodyweight exercises (such as lunges and push-ups), free weights (barbells and hand weights), resistance bands (rubber tubing)—and can be done without a gym membership. Generally, perform lower repetitions when using higher weights and vice versa. Many studies support regular strength training as an ideal way to decrease body fat and build muscle.

- **Walking:** Thirty minutes of leisurely to moderate-intensity daily walking can have a huge impact on health; this often-overlooked exercise has been shown to decrease depression and anxiety. Begin with ten to fifteen minutes per day, increasing time on your feet as you become more comfortable.

- **Kegel exercises:** Unless you've had a baby, you may not have heard of this muscle-building pelvic floor exercise, which strengthens the bladder, uterus, small intestine, and rectum. Kegel exercises are important; as muscles weaken with pregnancy and age, the muscles prevent fluid and gas leaks. Because they involve internal muscle contractions, you can exercise while seated, lying down, or even standing in line at the store.

* * *

Adding any of these exercises into your daily routine would reap health benefits in a matter of days. But there's more to the exercise equation than weekly workouts. Did you know that exercise can help you think?

Periodic exercise breaks boost mental skills. No matter your line of work, ten minutes of movement each hour can have huge implications on overall daily effectiveness. What kind of exercise are we talking about? You could go for a walk, jump on a stationary bike, or use a treadmill. You could do some light calisthenics, such as jumping jacks, squats, or whatever else comes to mind. What matters is movement, which increases blood flow to the brain. And that whatever you choose makes you happy—exercise programs should be fun, easy to get the hang of, and fit nicely within our schedule, applicable to what we do and enjoy. That workout should feel good, especially if we want to stick to it.

What are some other ways to encourage a regular exercise habit? Two things come to mind: friends and results. Most activities are more enjoyable with a friend, and exercise is no exception: a workout buddy can help you stick to a schedule. An exercise partner keeps the activity fun, prevents boredom, and provides accountability. If your routine is uninteresting or burdensome, chances are you won't stick to it. So, find a buddy and get to it. Results are certainly motivating—but many exercise benefits are internal and some find patience difficult. That's not to say you won't immediately reap results from your new exercise program. Through my personal experience and observation of thousands of patients and clients, I know observable results are possible after a single exercise session. The body is eager for movement, and you'll be shocked by how good you feel after fifteen to thirty minutes of basic exercise. The key is *observation*. Bringing The Process to exercise—being mindful in that movement—is key to recognizing results. Keep a log to record all the good things each workout accomplishes: improvements in skin, sleep, energy, and mood as well as gains in ability. And yes, weight loss, though the scale should never be our sole measure of exercise success.

Once you've implemented some basic exercises and become comfortable in a routine, the next step is increasing your intensity.

What I mean by intensity is the exertion of the workout—how hard or how long you're exercising.

Just like the rest of The Process, exercise is about your journey. It's unique and life-long, so be thankful you've started on this path and celebrate progress as you go!

CREATING HEALTHY EATING HABITS

The other component to physically *living better* is food. Of all our "daily musts," what we choose to eat is probably one of the most challenging. Healthy meals take planning: work in the kitchen, time at the grocery store, research in restaurants, and more. For some of us, this thoughtful approach is second nature because we've seen it modeled. But not everyone grew up in a house where parents were able to demonstrate healthy meal planning. Poor food choices create a downward spiral, including a myriad of health problems—diabetes, heart disease, kidney failure, cancer, and many other diseases attributed to misguided nutritional choices.

You may be confused by all the information on health and nutrition. I agree; it's hard to sift through all the stuff we're told is good (or bad) for us. From the latest fad diet to sugar substitutes and zero-calorie fountain drinks and whether eating organic fruits, vegetables, and meats is best—options and opinions are so varied they make the head spin. What one expert says today may seem like profound truth and yet, a year later, another expert says the same thing is harmful. Dizzy with confusion, no wonder it's difficult to figure out what's best for *you*.

While I cannot fix this, I can provide some solutions that will make healthy food choices a little easier. And when life is easier, good things follow—like saving some time and money, feeling better, and having a little extra pep in your step.

EATING MINDFULLY

When it comes to healthy eating, let's go slow. I'm talking about how fast you consume food. Did you know that the speed at which you eat is just as important as the type of food you are eating? It's true—slow is better for you. People ingest less food (and, often, fewer calories); digestion is better. There's less stress with a leisurely meal.

Sadly, in today's nonstop world, eating slowly is not so simple. There's nothing like living with children to illustrate this point. Once Danika and I had another mouth or two to feed, we instantly felt rushed. Someone else needed feeding; there were spills or vomit to clean up; under that pressure, we lost sight of leisurely enjoying a meal.

My youngest daughter, Siena, abhors being rushed for anything. At six years old, she asked why we ate dinner so quickly. Her question crushed me; dinnertime is often my only opportunity to sit with my family and listen to them talk about their day. As my child pointed out, rushing through that meal, our family time, was bad—for my inner health, my Core and Heart. I was moved; her childish observation was more profound than anything I'd learned in medical school.

If a six-year-old feels rushed at dinner, that's a wake-up call: I need to better incorporate mindfulness at my Table.

MEAL PLANNING

Though I thought I had meal planning down rather well, John Berardi, PhD (co-founder of Precision Nutrition, an exercise-based nutritional coaching business providing education and certification) made it even better. Dr. Berardi has helped thousands of people—including me—reinvent their bodies and lives through better nutrition.

A friend introduced me to Precision Nutrition in 2010. I began reading about Dr. Berardi's methodology and decided to test his theories myself. My results were so impressive that, in 2013, I took Precision Nutrition's course to become a certified nutrition specialist; in 2014, certification in hand, I began sharing information on diet and exercise with my patients. Since then, more than fifty have gone through the Precision Nutrition methodology and achieved a combined weight loss of nearly one thousand pounds!

Precision Nutrition teaches that, with some simple meal preparation and planning, you can make great food-based changes to your health. Even if you're new to cooking. As we'll discuss further, you don't need a lot—a few containers, assorted kitchen appliances—to successfully manage this essential part of *living better*.

MAKING GOOD FOOD

If we want to achieve sustainable health and happiness, food preparation is key. I'm not going to give you exact instructions: what, when, or how (cooked, raw, juiced). That's better left to other publications. Given our unique DNA profiles and varied schedules, there's no one way; our nutritional needs are individual (caveat: none of us really needs all that sugar). Instead, here's some basic tips for better eating:

Set a designated preparation day. A few hours in the kitchen enriches life in many ways. Lots of creativity emerges—we discover new food pairings, create satiating dishes, and enjoy emotional fulfillment (especially Danika, my wife). Investing in a few kitchen items—blender, Crock-Pot, zester, grater, and whatever else suits your fancy—adds ease and excitement to cooking. With one set day to accomplish the week's cooking, grocery shopping and kitchen clean up become more efficient. Plus, you have to plan!

Embrace leftovers. I'm a fan and, if you aren't already, I urge you to become one, too. Leftovers are a great time saver and huge problem solver. When you're creating in the kitchen, have some containers on hand to store prepped food; that way, healthy options are ready whenever you need to pack a lunch or grab a quick meal on a busy day. When leftovers or prepared meals are waiting in your fridge or freezer, it's easier to make better food choices.

Eat your veggies. Now, I said I wasn't going to tell you exactly what to eat. However, I advise lots of vegetables; the vitamins, minerals, and fiber veggies contain cannot be matched. Always have them at your disposal. Fresh or frozen doesn't matter; nutrient content of frozen veggies compares well to garden-fresh counterparts. Add some veggie chopping into your weekly prep day to make those multiple daily servings truly handy.

Choose fruit. While we can live without them, many fruits are good for us. Blueberries, for example, are low calorie, nutrient dense, and don't cause the large insulin spikes that can lead to diabetes. When shopping, choose colorful fruits—those pigments provide various cancer-fighting phytonutrients.

Supplement with protein powder. Easily digestible protein powders are available in a variety of types (whey or vegetable-based; for vegetarians, vegans, and omnivores) and provide muscle-building nutrients. A small serving mixed with water will not only assist muscle recovery after a workout but also help you feel full longer and avoid carbohydrate "crashes" from sugar-laden snacks and meals.

Make meal prep fun. Listen to an audio book, watch TV, put on some tunes—the possibilities are endless. Kitchen time can be joyous. If you have children, get them involved, and, if they make a mess, so be it—take some pictures for the family scrapbook. These are the moments that define our lives. Teach them how to cook and plan meals and they will thank you later.

MANAGING YOUR TIME AT THE SUPERMARKET

You have lots of other things to do in life that provide you more fulfillment than grocery shopping. Again, some planning can save time and provide better results. With a few modifications, you can even apply some of those tips I provided earlier:

Set a shopping schedule. I recommend going once or twice a week.

Know your menu. Go back to our discussion on healthy eating and having one food prep day. How do you know what to shop for and how to prep if you haven't planned your menu? Allow time in the schedule to decide what the week's meals will be well before your shopping and prep days.

Plan your list. Consult recipes for the ingredients needed to prepare the meals you've planned. Organize your list, preferably in conjunction with the store's layout. For example, arrange spatially (start at one end of the store and work your way through to the other). Or group by types of food (meats, produce, dairy, etc.).

Think strategically. If you're like me, you may like to shop at various markets. Consider your route and schedule options. Maybe it makes sense to shop all in one day; maybe strategically spacing out shopping makes sense, so you can go on your way home from work or to pick up the kids. Perhaps dividing and conquering is your best bet—you do some shopping while your partner does the other

There's a lot of wiggle room with food preparation and healthy eating. Key concept—be efficient. Advance planning provides many benefits, and keeping your refrigerator and pantry full of nutritious options means you'll always have something to look forward to. That's what I call a win-win.

EATING OUT

Healthy eating doesn't just happen at home. I don't want to forget mentioning eating out. Whether rich and poor, lots of us eat out multiple times a week. Perhaps eating out often is due to work and school demands, inability to shop for and store groceries, or dislike of cooking. No one's here to judge. I just want to help you become a health-conscious consumer.

Eating out may be a daily or weekly routine; perhaps you're traveling for work or looking for a way to relax. Whatever the circumstances for restaurant dining or picking up fast food, try to select healthy items with plenty of fresh vegetables. Look for protein and grains. Consider size; restaurant portions are often much larger than recommended, so opt for dividing your entree and saving some for the next day (leftovers!).

ABSOLUTE FOCUS: THE JORDAN KUNASZYK STORY

I remember that October, one of my favorite months in 2017, as if it were yesterday. That month, I had two detailed talks with Jordan Kunaszyk, Golden Bears linebacker. Jordan and I discussed having the proper mindset.

We'd met earlier, around October 9, when Jordan came to the UC Berkeley locker room to say hello. From his unwavering eye contact and inquisitive facial expression, he was clearly seeking something; within seconds of our handshake and hellos, he spoke about the injury that had sidelined him since the season's first game.

In September, the team had won a close victory on the road against the University of North Carolina. Still, coaches had told Jordan he was too focused on the injury; that nagging hamstring injury, they said, was continuing to mar his effectiveness. Playing linebacker takes brawn and brains, and Jordan wasn't functioning at the level the team needed for him to be effective on the field.

As we talked on that early October day, however, I could tell Jordan was seeking something more than medical advice. So, we scheduled another talk for October 17.

I learned a lot from Jordan. How belief and adversity had gotten him to UC Berkeley. How football was what he loved to do more than anything else. How his dream was to make it to the NFL. Yes, he'd let an injury dominate his mind. Yes, he likely could've been playing at a higher level earlier in the season. Something, I felt, was clouding his purpose.

If October 17 would turn out to be one of 2017's best days, those preceding it were quite sobering. An onslaught of fires ravaged Northern California, the coastal area known as the Redwood Empire. People evacuated their houses; one of the Golden Bears' players watched in agony as his family's home burned. Talks of canceling the football game against Washington State University dominated the news.

On Friday, October 13, the sky above Berkeley's Memorial Stadium was filled with smoke and ash, but the game was on. Jordan played; he and the rest of the team had an amazing game—the defense forced seven turnovers and nine sacks against the undefeated eighth-ranked NCAA team in the country. Jordan was named Pacific-12 Conference and National Defensive Player of the Week.

Between when we'd first met in the locker room and that night's game, Jordan's mindset had indeed changed. Was there a direct relationship? I'd like to think so but there's simply no proof in that. At the game, Jordan had thanked me for my words; the next day, he'd sent a more personal text message. I was elated at making a connection. In some way, The Process had helped. Perhaps our brief conversation inspired a stronger belief in himself. Perhaps I coached a new mindset, one less burdened by his injury. Perhaps I merely reinforced what he'd known all along.

I believe what happened at that game was the result of Jordan's absolute focus: his vision and expectations were clear, his attention to detail and solid decisions unwavering.

What I know for sure is that, because Jordan chose his path, something good happened. I just happened to be there. And to think he came to learn something from me.

IMPLEMENTING CHANGE: TAKING A PATIENT FROM DISEASE TO HEALTH

Change is one of the most difficult things humans encounter. Entire books have been written on the subject—from making slow changes to instant changes that have a huge impact on your life. I don't profess to have unlocked the secret; I want to help you assess your current health and well-being so you can implement changes for the better.

As a family medicine physician, I have an amazing opportunity—I'm directly involved in caring for people. Healthy and sick, young and the old, knowing my patients inside and out, I see health care as a privilege extending to the greatest depths of the soul. Sometimes, I may be the only listening ear they have. Helping others is a vocation I consider a calling.

The hardest part of this calling is persuading a patient to make lifestyle changes that may not provide visible results very quickly. Most physicians would probably agree with me. Often, the other thing that prompts a change to diet and activity level is the threat of death. Even then, patients are consistently anxious about and afraid of the challenges they may face and the failures that may arise with these changes.

I studied diligently to find something that would work. The Process wasn't part of medical school curricula (at least, not on the surface). I knew every patient and situation would be different and that even the smallest differences would complicate finding that secret recipe—that single prescription shifting the paradigm from poor decision-making to effective change and taking my patients from disease to health.

One day in my first year of residency, a patient arrived in my clinic. In his late thirties, this man was different from most of the active-duty men and women I was seeing in his age group—he worked as a police officer for the Veterans Affairs Health Clinic; his spouse was the active duty Air Force officer.

While visiting family during a vacation, he began to feel ill. He described it as feeling "off," as if he'd eaten something that didn't agree with him very well. Then one night, he began sweating profusely. Minutes later, his vision blurred and he became confused. A family member brought him to a nearby emergency room, where he was resuscitated with intravenous fluids and connected to an array of cardiac and pulmonary monitors. His blood was drawn and tests run. It didn't take long to figure out the problem: hyperglycemia, otherwise known as high blood sugar.

People who are hyperglycemic do not process insulin properly, and my patient's organs were essentially shutting down. He would now be classified as diabetic, a disease that many health care professionals often consider irreversible. Why? Most of the time, patients aren't willing to sacrifice their current lifestyle and diet to reverse the condition.

By the time he'd come to my clinic, this patient had been prescribed a once-per-day medication to help his body's resistance to insulin. I rechecked his sugar levels—they were off the chart. Clearly, he needed more than an oral medication; nothing short of daily insulin injections would halt his body's deterioration. I was furious that the hospital hadn't offered this critical treatment, but I didn't let my anger detract from the issue at hand.

This family man had a respectable, well-paying job that required day and night shifts and carrying a firearm. One important requirement: he had to be free from any health problems that could interfere with duties, most specifically carrying his weapon. He needed an answer to his new nightmare—could I help? I was extremely nervous; I hadn't had such a young patient with such an advanced progression of this disease. Could I correct the severity of his disease? I'd do whatever I could. As I created a plan, I knew the only way to make it work was with his direct input.

Just shorter than six feet tall, my patient weighed in at 250 pounds. First, I adjusted his medication, increasing the ER's original dosage to twice daily. I also added a hefty dose of insulin injected into the skin and tissue covering his abdomen each night before bed. Second, the two of us constructed a plan for weight loss. Dropping extra pounds would not only improve quality of life and decrease risk of complications from diabetes but also alleviate some knee pain he'd been experiencing. Third (but not least), we discussed his need to quit smoking.

Within six months, my patient was feeling better. He'd stopped smoking. He was eating better, swapping most of the empty calories he'd been consuming (potato chips and candy) with healthy fats and protein. At this point, he'd lost fifteen pounds; his serum blood markers, which show the amount of free floating sugar in the blood, had vastly improved.

Another six months passed before I saw my patient again, nearly one year since our first visit. He had absolutely no tobacco cravings. Now, he was running at least thirty minutes every day. He'd lost nearly forty pounds. His knees felt better (yes, this can happen when you start running). But he was anxious and concerned. He didn't understand why his weight loss had plateaued; he was doing everything we'd written up in his plan. In the last two months, however, he hadn't shed a single pound and he wanted to lose at least ten more.

I decided to combat his plateau on several fronts. I decreased his medications, turned off the insulin (because insulin is a growth hormone, I was concerned it was causing some weight gain, since he was exercising and replacing body fat with lean muscle), and decreased the dosage of his medication. We know how important mindset is to The Process so, to fuel his motivation, I gave him a book—something I'd found in the clinic, on a random bookshelf, about the "bucket of life" and keeping goals from fading. I incorporated basic weight-lifting into his plan (twenty- to thirty-minute workouts, two to three times per week).

Three months later, my patient had lost five more pounds. He was now five pounds shy of his fifty-pound weight-loss goal, and his blood markers showed him as "prediabetic" (a term that means glucose levels, while higher than normal, are less than the range of diabetes). Having lost one-fifth of his body weight, he appeared to be a new man.

Six months later, the man returned for a follow-up. His exam and numbers looked great. Hopeful that we had reversed his disease, I adjusted his medication to a single pill per day. My patient said he was feeling the best he had in twenty years.

What, I wondered, made this patient different from so many others I'd seen in my practice? How had he handled dramatic changes to his diet and exercise so well? After much reflection, I decided the reason this plan worked was because it was *his* plan, not mine. Instead of handing him some instructions (which the bulk of patients often throw away before leaving the clinic), I'd coached him to make his own decisions. I hadn't told what worked for me or gave directions. Instead, he became more self-aware and instituted self-control, developing knowledge that allowed him to get back up each time he suffered a setback. In short, I helped him create his Process.

This patient often said to me, "If I could do what I have done, then I am certain anyone else can do the same. You kept talking about The Process, Dr. V., and while it took me a while to understand what you were saying, I totally get it now." The Process, a philosophy that built my life's work, was having an effect in more ways than I'd ever imagined.

Don't wait to make changes—the right time is now, before something goes wrong with your health. My patient clearly demonstrated that where there is a will, there is a way. Though you likely possess all the tools you'll need for success, if you need some help or motivation to begin improving your mind and body, keep reading. I'm confident you'll be making those changes before you realize it.

END-OF-CHAPTER ASSESSMENT

Are you thinking more about your health and living better? Have you been inspired to take the necessary steps to effect change in your mind and body?

Now you know that a little exercise goes a long way and there's no need to force activity you don't enjoy. Hopefully, this chapter has you thinking about what you eat and the types of foods in your grocery cart. You learned a few tips for better meal planning and food preparation. With *Exceptional Every Day*, you've got an easy-to-use tool kit at your disposal. If taking care of your mind and body were not priorities in the past, there's no excuse for that kind of thinking now. Let's get on with the next steps so you can reap the healthy rewards waiting for you.

Questions for Reflection and Direction

Before moving on to the next chapter, take a moment to answer the following questions, either in the space provided or your journal. When you're ready, I'll meet you in Chapter 8.

THE PROCESS CHECKLIST

Priority 7: Your Mind and Body

1. How do you feel when you wake up each morning?

_____

_____

_____

2. What do you know about the benefits of exercise?

_____

_____

_____

3. List three small dietary changes you can make this week.

_____

_____

_____

4. What do you believe are the consequences of living an inactive life?

_____

_____

_____

5. For the next five days, keep a workout and food diary. Share what you learned (you may be surprised at how much more mindful you are of food and exercise habits when you track them in this way).

_____

_____

_____

8 HONORING SPIRITUALITY AND THE SOUL

"Faith is taking the first step, even when you don't see the whole staircase."
—Dr. Martin Luther King, Jr.

If there were ever a topic that makes many people uneasy, it would have to be spirituality. Perhaps you say *faith*, *religion*, or *belief system*; you'll find I use these terms interchangeably. Regardless of the wording, spiritual practice is an important part of life. I'm not intending to give a sermon, deliver a lecture, or discuss the Bible, Koran, Torah, or any other book professing faith. Instead, I'm looking to reinforce where believers may currently be in their spiritual life while offering perspective for those who are indecisive or indifferent about this topic. Spirituality is simply a word. But the concept may provide an answer to the many problems we encounter with the overall flow of our Process. For those of you who think spirituality is confined to a religion, stick around; I think you'll be pleasantly surprised. There is something here for all of us.

Whether five minutes each morning or four hours on Sunday (shout-out to all my Mormon friends), a consistent and solid spiritual practice can be one of the most important and integral elements in managing your life. John Calipari, the University of Kentucky men's head basketball coach, attends Catholic mass every day at 0800. That's his thing. It's what makes him tick, something he not only attributes as part of his success but also sees as a life management tool. Remember: life management is what The Process is really after. While no one has to practice a religion, you do have to be *you*—and every soul benefits from a little sprinkling of spirituality. This one nourishing part of our Process can have huge implications.

A FATHER'S FAITH: SIENA'S STORY

Look, I get it. Some of you who don't profess to be spiritual may be thinking about tuning out right now. You must trust me when I tell you that spirituality is only religious if you choose so. I'd like to highlight this with my own story, one that's hardly religious but has everything to do with faith in The Process and believing in something bigger than yourself.

Before our youngest daughter was born, my wife and I struggled with finding that perfect name. We were stuck, going back and forth (after all, naming your child doesn't really involve a do-over) before finally deciding on her first name—Siena. But I wanted something more, a middle name (Danika was more focused on pregnancy and raising our older child, two things that can be rather unforgiving of your time).

I wanted Siena's middle name to be something unique, something I'd never heard in my thirty years of life. While connecting to my roots, the name should also grant Siena her individuality. Its meaning could help her transcend obstacles she'd encounter on her journey through life. Danika saw how driven I was, and she allowed me to proceed with my conviction. And then the name finally came to me. We would call her "Imani," which means "faith" in Swahili.

Siena Imani first said a stoic hello to us—not a single cry—on March 7, 2012. Late in the morning hours of March 8, we'd learn the impact her middle name would have on me, my family, and our friends. We were at the Medical College of Wisconsin (I was in the middle of my medical education there, having invested nearly two years of my life, with two more to go, in procuring my degree), and, just twenty-four hours after Siena was born, I had returned to my wife's postpartum room to learn she'd failed the initial hearing screening.

I was naïve about what that meant; at this point in my medical training, I hadn't studied much of anything to do with hearing. The nurses assured me the failure was most likely due to a mechanical error. Danika and I weren't too worried, that is, until the next day, when Siena failed the hearing test again. Still, we were told the results were most likely an error—six infants had failed the same test in the past week. The screening technician explained fault could lie with the machine or amniotic fluid in the baby's ears. The pediatrician on-call determined more tests were needed and put in an order for a kidney ultrasound, as hearing loss is often related to various syndromes. The radiologist didn't find anything remarkable on the kidney ultrasound, so there was no explanation for the failed test.

While preparing to be discharged from the hospital and looking forward to returning to the comforts of our home, Siena's doctor asked us to schedule a repeat test with the children's audiology clinic in two weeks. Danika and I were in limbo, beyond stressed, and quite apprehensive about what would happen next. Our faith in God and the medical system were being tested in more ways than one. However, I knew that having faith could be as simple as believing that what you want to happen will.

Due to the rigors of medical school, I had to miss the follow-up appointment.

Danika called, hysterical and sobbing: Siena had once again failed the hearing test. As if that weren't bad enough, during the evaluation, the nurse made comments about possible illicit drug use during pregnancy—you can imagine how Danika felt about that. (A third adult in the room, an audiologist, verified everything, and let's just say it did not end well.) Could this scenario get any worse?

Danika said the audiologist wanted to follow up in six months. *Six months?* I was livid—hell, no! Six months of waiting was *not* going to work for me. Retesting had to be *now*, not later. I seethed. Questions rocked my brain. Why was my God doing this? How could the medical system I was striving so diligently to join not make infant hearing a priority? Why was our faith being tested so? I was lucky to have knowledge on my side, but what about all those parents in similar situations who don't? How do families in our position—parents whose newborn has unexplained issues—cope when they don't know to ask the right questions?

Siena couldn't fight for herself. Those other parents out there, going through similar agony, couldn't do it alone. But my beliefs would provide the strength I needed to take on these challenges. In this moment, my Process crystallized.

Determined to get answers fast, I called a mentor at the children's hospital for advice and support. We talked; afterward, my mentor called Dr. David Beste, an otolaryngologist friend, who contacted me immediately. Could we get Siena to his office before the end of the day? Yes, we could. At the office, Dr. Beste quickly snatched the insurance forms from my hand, ripping them apart and throwing them away, asking only that I "pay it forward" (meaning, once I became a physician, to do the same selfless deed for someone else.

I can honestly say I've followed that order whenever possible—and it feels good).

During the examination, Dr. Beste couldn't find anything physically wrong with Siena's ears. No missing eardrums, the ear canals were patent (open), and there was no fluid. From a visual standpoint, Siena's ears appeared normal. He told us not to fret and arranged for an appointment with an audiologist in ten days, much sooner than the six-month follow-up our other doctor had proposed.

I admired Dr. Beste for his intentional practice, following through with his words, and bringing as much closure as he could to his patients. His Process was laid out before me; he wanted to live up to his last name by providing the *best* care possible.

Those were ten long days, though. With a two-year-old and newborn at home, attention spans were limited and we grew impatient. But the appointment finally came, and this test was a little different. It took place in a small, dark room; there were a bunch of wires and equipment; and the test took three hours, much longer than the previous twenty-minute tests. I watched the audiologist like a hawk, trying to assess her reaction to every waveform on the screen. What was wrong and how bad was Siena's situation?

As the audiologist broke the news, our hearts and spirits were crushed. Siena had moderate to profound hearing loss in both ears. She would require hearing aids, possible further intervention, and perhaps never speak coherently. I was beyond devastated—I felt like I'd been run over by a truck. My faith in the medical world and God was eroding, my admiration for a higher being dwindling. I felt stranded, alone on an island of despair. You see, Danika and I have no experience with hearing loss; we have no family members with this condition. There was no defined reason our baby did not have normal hearing, and that troubled me most.

At home after the appointment, I was a mess. Needing time to sort myself out, I walked the neighborhood alone. And then, like a scared, lost child, I stopped at Jared Forrester's apartment. My friend invited me in; at first I was ashamed to share the feelings that had brought me to his door, but Jared's compassion and empathy reminded me that my higher power often places others in our path to help us navigate life's obstacles.[5] Even though we might forget it at times, God is good.

Our family had no choice but to press forward with our lives. Yes, Siena's hearing loss tested our faith; it did not, however, destroy it. The Process was in motion. Now was the time for acceptance, not wishing for change—this was our baby, our gift.

I've come to see that, as Siena's life evolves, she will require a little help for something most of us take for granted. And as I look back on my quest to find my daughter's perfect middle name, I realize that "faith" was no coincidence.

SPIRITUALITY: A HISTORICAL PERSPECTIVE

Looking back in time through the lens of war surely illustrates the good and the bad that can come from being too religious or spiritual. Throughout time, the world has been marred by wars, and, on the surface, causes of these conflicts appear to be the result of politics, ego, narcissism, and money. But if you peel away the layers, you'll see religion is often the major culprit in war and unrest.

From Israel to Germany, the United States to Japan, and countries bordering the Arabian Gulf, war has been a constant. Even now, as I write this, the U.S. has conducted its second airstrike in twelve months, more than one hundred missiles launched into Syria from ships, submarines, and aircraft. I won't argue with the presumed reason for action against the Assad regime—a recent chemical weapons

---

5   It's no wonder I sought Jared out. That empathy and compassion have led him to become an amazing physician and surgeon who's given part of his life to others less fortunate in Ethiopia, where hope often fails to thrive, with the nonprofit Lifebox.

attack killed thousands of innocent people, including many women and children. For nearly eighteen years, I've honored the serviceman's oath I swore to follow the President of the United States' orders. But I'm also an independent thinker, and my concern is that a counterattack predisposes continued attacks: America is contributing to, rather than solving, Syria's problems. And interwoven in the roots of this issue, going back thousands of years, lies religion.

FINDING INSPIRATION

Religion offers a sense of inspiration, something beyond anything we can feel or observe. The feeling religion fosters transcends obstacles, allows freedom and the ability to dream, and gives comfort beyond measure. When hope is low or grief is constant, when nothing seems to be working out, religion may be all we have. Many people need this reassurance and assistance daily to help them get by.

Call that feeling whatever you want—there's no need to put any sort of label on it. If you're moved and there's positive flow, go for it. Yes, books and "prophets" will try to persuade and sell you on a certain religion; I want to show you that religion transcends labels, belief systems, and places to hang out at on Sunday mornings. What truly matters is not the form of practice but the inspiration a belief provides.

END-OF-CHAPTER ASSESSMENT

If you stuck around to hear me share the value of having a spiritual life, I commend you. That idea is often a hard pill to swallow. Separating spirituality (or faith, or religion—remember, we're not getting hung up on the label) from a form of practice makes it much easier for many to see that belief is instrumental in our lives. Do you believe that what you want is indeed possible? That feeling can move you to new heights and help you overcome some of life's most challenging obstacles. Spirituality is not limited to belief in some God or higher being—it's a beneficial feeling available to every one of us.

Questions for Reflection and Direction

As you prepare to move to the next section, take a moment to digest what spirituality means to you. Then, answer the questions in the space provided or in your own journal. When you're ready, I'll meet you in Chapter 9.

THE PROCESS CHECKLIST

Priority 8: Spirituality and the Soul

1. Do you believe in something beyond yourself? If so, describe it. If not, why not?

_____

_____

_____

2. Do you think your Process could benefit from digging deeper into this realm?

_____

_____

_____

3. Think about people in your life who have a spiritual life. What qualities, and/or characteristics do they share?

_____

_____

_____

4. What do you think would happen if you made spirituality a priority in your life? If it already is, what could improve your spiritual life?

_____

_____

_____

9 EMBRACING REST, PLAY, AND SLEEP

"Life is all about balance. You don't always need to be getting stuff done. Sometimes it's perfectly okay, and absolutely necessary, to shut down, kick back and do nothing."

—Lori Deschene

Have you ever considered how little time you spend resting? Daily, it seems as if we're all sprinting; life, however, is truly more of a marathon. We don't often take a break to smell the roses (literally) and listen to the birds. To-do lists pile up; day after day, we check off one item only to add two or three more. Have you smiled or laughed today?

It's easy to disregard rest and play as essential to well-being, especially when we're responsible for others. In the triage of today's hurried world, our own health and wellness is often shoved to the rear.

Think back to Chapter 1. I'd like to remind you of its lesson—you are indeed your top priority. There's a reason for that: you can only serve others by first living for yourself. Is this selfish? I used to think so, but that's hardly the case. You must know yourself and take care of yourself to do good work, and finding time for rest is an essential component in self-care. This chapter illustrates cultivating balance by carving out time each day to replenish yourself.

THE NEED FOR REST

Sprinting through life is not an option. The human body only makes and stores so much adenosine triphosphate (ATP), the enzyme that allows us to perform short and powerful bursts of activity. This enzyme lasts only seconds, not minutes or hours. There's always something to be done, and I'm as guilty as anyone else—we don't rest enough. Have you stopped to consider that resting deserves a spot on that to-do list? If, like me, you hope to achieve a life of prosperity, then finding ways to relax and play are very important. You cannot enjoy The Process without accepting the idea of rejuvenation.

Correcting and maximizing this priority can't happen overnight. Depending on how much damage all that sprinting has caused, learning how to relax or play may take a great deal of work and time. Believe me—you're going to need to invest the same (if not more) amount of desire and motivation into the fun stuff as you're putting into other priorities.

MODERATE DOESN'T MEAN MEDIOCRE

I used to think *moderation* was synonymous with *mediocrity*. I had no concept of moderation; my friends and teammates used to say, "Go big or go home," and that was the way I wanted to live. Over time, however, I witnessed repercussions of that "go big or go home" attitude: addictions, injuries (for others and within myself), and stress. My thoughts changed when I began to see what moderation could offer my life. Moderation allowed me to take breaks and reflect. It allowed recovery from injuries. It allowed better digestive health (not feeling bloated or sick to my stomach after a meal). Most of all, it allowed me time to do more of the important things in life.

I won't lie: this growth process was very frustrating. My life needed more moderation, and accepting that moderation did not equal mediocrity took a great deal of patience. After getting knocked down a few times, I started to see that embracing moderation could make me *better*.

Are you an overachiever, someone who cannot figure out how to pump the brakes? Trying some moderation will help realign your priorities; your whole life will benefit from not overdoing it. Applying basic rules can aid you in this readjustment. The following is a short list of some things that have helped me prioritize rest and relaxation:

1. Stop. Take breaks from the action. If you don't, you might miss something important.

2. Make a list of things you enjoy doing. Then, make time to do them.

3. Get enough sleep. This is when your body grows and repairs itself.

4. Reassess things you think *need* to get done. Then, see #2.

5. Respect your time by not giving it away to everyone who demands it.

SLEEP

One major component of rest is sleep. Research has shown sleep to be the most efficient way to improve our health; in fact, extreme sleep deprivation is the main reason for premature death.[6] Perhaps, like me, you struggle with finding time to sleep. Perhaps some medical or unknown etiology keeps you from sleeping well. My wife is lucky; sleep comes easily to Danika (and sleeping in, even easier). She's mastered this priority! Though I'm not usually the envious type, I must admit I wish I possessed some of her mastery. While some people (like Danika) are natural sleepers, others (like me) struggle with it nightly. In my nightly search for good sleep, I've tried multiple modalities only to come up empty, trial after trial—and I'm a family medicine physician.

I've tried a mixture of over-the-counter zinc and magnesium (it's done some good but isn't foolproof). At night, I've banned television, computer usage, or any type of screen time you can think of. I don't consume any caffeine. I've adjusted food and drink, suspending fluid intake and eliminating heavy meals from a minimum of two hours before my head hits the pillow. I've tried icy cold and scalding hot showers. I've used a white noise machine at night and a HappyLight in the morning. I've adjusted workout times, trying multiple workouts with severe calorie restriction (in the same day) to see if being more tired would help me sleep. Unfortunately, none of these techniques have offered me much relief. (What I haven't tried is prescription medication. Once, while I was working a mess of days and night in the ER, someone ordered me some Ambien. I brought the bottle home, where it sat in my cupboard, unopened, for twelve months. I finally threw it away.)

As hard as I've tried, the recommended amount of sleep (eight hours) isn't something I can do. I wish it worked for me, but six hours appears to be my normal. When I sleep that long, I wake up feeling good and ready to take on the day. I've learned what my body needs. Perhaps you are similar. All of us should find what

6   https://www.nhlbi.nih.gov/health-topics/sleep-deprivation-and-deficiency.

works and maximize sleep efficiency; save the bedroom for rest and sex. Turn down those lights and shut off those screens. If you're having trouble falling asleep (or staying asleep), get up, do something relaxing for a bit, and then give the bedroom another try.

Rest is part of The Process and a crucial investment in yourself. How we spend the day's precious seconds often defines the value of our nights. If you can better manage your sleep, you'll find more energy and time to achieve goals and dreams.

ACTIVE REST: TAKING TIME OUT TO PLAY

As we've discussed in this chapter, rest is an important and often ignored component in The Process. Most Processes fail due to this improper prioritizing. Taking time for rest in its various forms doesn't mean you're lazy. Or that you're failing to move toward your goals or stay within your Process. While sleep is an important part of rest, play (sometimes called *active rest*) is another way to recharge.

Play means different things to different people: going out with friends, playing tennis, spending time with family, scheduling time for a hobby you like. Most general practitioners would argue that sex is a form of active rest; hormones released during lovemaking create a state of homeostasis (repair).

The human body needs down time, where we function at a lower energy expenditure level, to grow and heal. The value of active rest is all around—at home, work, in the gym, and anywhere you look—in the energy and quality of life we gain. To reap those rewards, each of us needs to find ways to rest that work and incorporate them into daily life.

REFLECT AND RESET

Another part of resting is our ability to handle stressors, tasks, and obligations. Whether you divert daily, withdraw weekly, or abandon annually, the way you achieve this mental relaxation means something different for each of us. This difference isn't what's important—that we *do it* is crucial. Giving our minds rest is just as important as giving our bodies rest.

One of the best ways to enjoy mental rest is in reflection. By this, I mean taking time to think about your life: where you've come from, the roads traveled, moments of adversity, and especially moments of joy. Most of us are unfamiliar with this broader meaning; self-reflection isn't something we're taught in school. We're more accustomed to a superficial reflection, what we see in the mirror while brushing our teeth, shaving, or putting on makeup. Many people marginalize how valuable self-reflection can be. Over the course of my life, I've come to believe this practice stands alone atop life's pedestal as a way to gain better perspective and achieve in life. It's hard to reflect when you're actively doing something else (is there really such a thing as "multitasking"?). When you're busy, it's nearly impossible to tap into that deep part of your mind and accomplish valuable reflection.

As one of our best and most precious mechanisms for growth, everyone should take some time (just five minutes a day) to sit in a quiet spot, free of distractions, such as the many screens that commandeer our attention or family members, friends, and coworkers who demand our time. Find somewhere to rest and quietly sit with yourself, alone at your Table.

At first, self-reflection may seem unnecessary. Perhaps you think you have your life all figured out. Maybe you say this practice is a waste of time. I disagree and have found the reverse to be true. Self-reflection is a valuable and restorative part of active recovery. So, give yourself the peace that comes with reflection. Do it now; do it tomorrow; do it often.

END-OF-CHAPTER ASSESSMENT

Rest is a low-stress activity, with a plethora of benefits, that's crucial to proper life management. If you didn't know it before, you now know that "resting" comes in various forms. Resting doesn't mean you're doing nothing; you're finding ways to give your mind and body a break from daily stress. Rest provides new opportunities for growth and renewal and helps you hone in on your purpose, passion, and goals. Self-reflection is quiet time, when you can turn inward and examine priorities. How can you incorporate more rest into your life? The tools you've learned in this chapter and activities that follow should help you get started.

Questions for Reflection and Direction

Before moving on to the next chapter, take a moment to answer the following questions, either in the space provided or your journal. When you're ready, I'll meet you in Chapter 10.

THE PROCESS CHECKLIST

Priority 9: Rest, Play, and Sleep

1. What do you currently do to rest?

_____

_____

_____

2. What would you rather be doing?

_____

_____

_____

3. How is your sleep; do you wake up refreshed? What changes would you like to see in this area of your life?

_____

_____

_____

4. Do you find time to play? How much more active relaxation could you realistically fit into your weekly schedule?

_____

_____

_____

5. Make a list of new activities you'd like to try weekly over the next one to three months.

_____

_____

_____

10 ALLOWING FOR SOMETHING BIGGER

"Ensure you have enough energy each day to make a difference in other people's lives."

—Tom Rath

ADDING VALUE TO OTHERS: LEE IACOCCA'S STORY

Think of your Process as an assembly line. As you grow, you contribute to the end product; it's what you add to life that matters.

This idea came to life as I lost myself in *Iacocca: An Autobiography*. I enjoyed learning about Lee Iacocca, the son of Italian immigrants. How he attended Lehigh University before working his way to the top of Ford Motor Company. At Ford, Mr. Iacocca made his employees and the company valuable by always focusing on "addition" and not being fixated on "subtraction."

When Henry Ford, Jr. fired him as the company's president, Mr. Iacocca was transitioned to a desolate office during his final months and forced to publicly announce his resignation rather than speak the truth. He was a man without a home.

Instead of dwelling on his loss, Mr. Iacocca knew it was time to focus on adding his own value. He reached out to Ford's staunch competitor, the Chrysler Company, for employment. Chrysler was in dire financial straits, on the brink of extinction, and Mr. Iacocca voluntarily cut his salary to a single dollar per year, a move that challenged his ambitious work ethic. It didn't take long before Chrysler was back on the automotive map.

Process improvement is what Mr. Iacocca sought; process in action is what he believed would drive Chrysler to success. Every day, leading his people and challenging them to create the best cars on the road, Lee Iacocca added value to life. As he reached toward something bigger, process was the name of his game. Make process the name of your game every day.

SUCCESS VS. SIGNIFICANCE

John C. Maxwell, an American author on leadership, once said, "Success is when I add value to myself. Significance is when I add value to others." I've often contemplated what being successful truly means, especially within the framework of technological advancements enabling faster and easier connections. For instance, how is someone with large numbers of Instagram followers "successful" if she cheated on her spouse while he was away defending their country? Or how can someone who's raking in millions still be considered iconic after having many dark secrets displayed to the public? I do believe people deserve a second chance (sometimes even a third, or more); as humans, we all make mistakes. But if you're confused about what defines *success*, chances are you're not alone.

In determining success, I've battled with my intentions, choices, and vision. I've refined values, and sought peace. Each day has brought new obstacles, experiences, and, most importantly, new opportunities for growth. The process has, without doubt, been a struggle.

This is my first book; my original topic was solely focused on time management. I soon realized I needed to include outcomes. Unless I found a way to talk about success and significance within this thing I called The Process, time management alone wouldn't be enough of a topic. Helping readers who were seeking a new way to define themselves—or perhaps revisiting an old way, with a new perspective—would give my book a chance to work. The pieces began to come together.

What's the timeline? Some have told me the first half of our lives—twenties, thirties, and forties—should be focused on becoming successful, working and socking away funds. The second half, then, is when we should strive for significance—retire at fifty and spend the second half of life giving to charities you believe in. That thinking would be fine and dandy (though somewhat boring), if each of us knew how long we were going to live. But we don't.

I read a book once on this specific idea; it targeted fifty-somethings (and older) who'd had a primary career and were looking for something more. It sold many copies, but my concern was that it wasn't aimed at a wide enough group of people—all those younger people who could also be looking to do something more were left out. I believe we can be *successful* and *significant* at the same time, independent of our decade or season of life. It's not about achieving great riches and then donating to charity, or working sixty-plus hours per week and then volunteering a few hours here and there. Significance can happen now, regardless of your age or accomplishments.

BECOMING SIGNIFICANT

Significance requires activity; you must do something. You may think it must be something grand or profound, but that's not the case. The reality is, you need only *do something*. Doesn't that take away a lot of pressure? You simply need to find something that moves you. Now, ask yourself: could what moves you have a positive and possibly life-altering effect on another person or group of people? If the answer is *yes*, go for it. That's how simple choosing a life of significance and achieving true happiness can be.

Significance starts with a single step. There's not much to contemplate—first, choose a direction (it may not even be the right direction, but don't worry—getting started is most important). Where to go with that first step? You could find an hour a week to help elementary students with reading (this always puts a smile on my face) or a couple of days a month preparing meals at a soup kitchen or battered women's shelter. Perhaps you could volunteer a few hours each week grocery shopping for elderly or disabled people who aren't able to get out on their own. The list of possibilities is endless.

Money—the idea that it takes money to make a difference—is another thing that often prohibits people from starting toward significance. I've fallen prey to this thinking; I'd tell myself I'd donate to this or that cause once there was more money in the bank. Somehow, I held tightly to the conviction that lots of money is needed to make a difference in the world. As I worked on my personal growth, however, I loosened that grip—significance doesn't require money. It takes desire.

Caring about something larger than yourself—The Process—is where significance starts. A single idea. A single vision. A picture in your mind. After that, add motion; take your priorities, make your time count, and let The Process flow. We miss many opportunities because we're overly focused on ourselves; that tunnel vision blinds us to how simple obtaining significance can be. It doesn't have to be this way—your opportunity to do something meaningful is likely right in front of you.

TIME MANAGEMENT

With all the homework you've had thus far it wouldn't surprise me to hear you're out of time—today's 86,400 seconds are gone and you don't have a single one left to spare. You might also tell me you're not ready for significance or something bigger than yourself; you're still working on *you*. I get it. But I'm going to let you in on a little secret: you will *always* be working on you.

Getting better or becoming exceptional every day is what this is all about, and when I say *every day*, I mean exactly that. It's not a metaphor for getting better once a month or even once a year. Working on improving yourself every single day is an attainable goal. So, now that we've gotten that out of the way, go ahead and remove this excuse from your list. It's not time that is against you; rather, it's your perception of time that's holding you back. One day—all 86,400 seconds of it—is a decent amount of time and if we had more, we'd surely fill that time with more obligations. Your boss would have you work longer hours. Your kids would be signed up for another lesson. Your friends and family would insist you help them with one more task. The cycle of being "too busy" would persist.

Instead of worrying about how much or how little time you have, focus on what's already available to you. How can you best use that time? Find something you can help with. Reach outside your comfort zone. Search for a place where you can make a difference. It may take a few tries to find the right thing, but eventually you'll land there. If your heart's in the game, time will work out. You don't need a whole lot of time. You hardly need any money.

I'd venture to say that, right now, you're as ready as you'll ever be to do something bigger and soon, you'll be serving to a capacity you never dreamed possible.

FINDING YOUR NICHE

Without realizing it, I wound up in a Mastermind Group. That's a fancy name for people working together to solve a problem; the expectation is that, by collaborating, they'll come up with a better solution than if they'd worked alone. Three of us made up this group: me, a business owner who was seeking coaching services for an employee, and a trauma therapist who'd been working with the company for a few years. During our conversation, I realized how much I truly love coaching people about personal growth. So many (including me) need help, but there's not enough time to help everyone. The key is zeroing in, finding a niche, and benefitting those you can.

HELPING THOSE IN NEED

Fighting for those who cannot fight for themselves is one of the quickest and easiest ways to become significant. Or by speaking up for those who have no voice. People in need are everywhere; they may live next door or share a cubicle at work. Maybe you see them on the street corner, waiting for the bus, or at the supermarket.

If you look for need, you'll find there are countless ways you can help. My friend Brendan and his family have been building new homes for families in need in Tijuana, Mexico, for the past ten years. When they show up, a cement slab awaits; the volunteers have about five days to build the house from the ground up, inside and out, which is no small task. They work all day and into the night and together, they create something that will surely provide comfort to a family in need.

Small acts can have outsized significance. I met a man in Vista, California, who exemplifies this. In 2018, Anthem Church was brand new and renting space at a local high school. Church leaders needed all the help they could get putting up and breaking down their equipment each Sunday. One day, this gentleman showed up; though he admitted he was not a "believer," something had called him to help. Every Sunday, from the time we met until the Navy called me to a new duty station, I watched this man gracefully set up and tear down classrooms for the children's ministry. The wonderful lessons my daughters were learning in those classrooms transformed that small, simple act of kindness into something much larger than one man.

Needy people aren't only on the receiving end of help; they seek significance, too. The Process matters just as much, but these poor people may have no idea how to begin. It's not that they're uneducated or lack insight. The problem is priorities.

Needy people are focused on surviving. They're worried about their next meal or whether there's money to pay the bills. Or maybe they're homeless and don't know when they'll have clean clothes to wear or comfortable beds to sleep in. Thoughts of success and significance are not on their radar; neither is reading this book or any of the thousands of others out there giving proclamations on getting ahead. I wish I could make those cares go away and show them how important working on *you* can be.

Everyone who makes the conscious decision to do so will become ready for significance. If you're reading this now, you're just seconds away. Keep diving in. Get your Process going. Know that, when your focus is on others—especially those who just don't have the capacity or ability to fight for themselves—your contribution makes a bigger impact than you might ever realize. So, there's no reason to wait; you are indeed needed, and that should be enough motivation to get started.

GETTING INVOLVED IS AS EASY AS 1-2-3

New opportunities abound once you've made a conscious decision to become significant. The journey starts with your character—knowing who you are, who you want to be, and which is your correct path. Combining each of your experiences to build upon passion and purpose provides the fuel you need to push forward.

The path, however, can be lonely and daunting. You can't become significant without a clear, defined Process, and we know that developing your Process is a daily commitment. You'll continually reevaluate decisions, planning, and goals; what works today may lead to very dismal results tomorrow. Life is full of the unexpected—sometimes, chaos feels like the only constant. We have no guarantees, and we have no control over others' decisions. The president of the United States might decide a new tax or medical insurance plan is best without considering the people's needs. A doctor prescribes medication for high blood pressure or diabetes without involving patients in the decision-making process; the boss assesses salary and number of vacation days without inviting employees' input. Things we feel content about may fall by the wayside in minutes. There's no choice but to keep moving, trusting that character and values will guide you past this tipping point. Trust in The Process will propel you to succeed, destroy complacency, and chart a course toward life's real value.

PAY IT FORWARD

Remember my daughter, Siena, and the good Dr. Beste? What an example—if you want to be significant, focus on "paying it forward." When someone does a good deed that you, in turn, pass on to another, you've paid the debt forward. There's a domino effect: as you become more proficient at managing your life, you're more in control of your Why. When you know your Why, you can help others find and develop theirs. That's truly paying it forward.

END-OF-CHAPTER ASSESSMENT

In this chapter, I shared some examples to inspire you to get out in the community and help others. We explored the difference between success and significance and how doing something beyond your-self—something that changes even one person's life for the better—is part of living a significant life. You don't have to be wealthy or retired, old or young, or educated with a special degree to make a difference. You have everything you need to be significant . . . and the time to act on your good intentions is *now*.

Questions for Reflection and Direction

Before moving on to the next chapter, take a moment to answer the following questions in the space provided or in your journal. When you're ready, I'll meet you in Chapter 11.

THE PROCESS CHECKLIST

Priority 10: Something Bigger Than You

1. List three societal issues that you think need help.

_____

_____

_____

2. Now, which of these problems can you help with today? What are you willing to give up in life to develop your significance?

_____

_____

_____

3. Pick one issue and reach out; contact someone or an organization currently working on making a difference to see how you can assist.

_____

_____

_____

4. After reviewing your priorities, build a calendar—where do you have gaps in your time? What are one or two things you can do to use that time to help others?

_____

_____

_____

5. Now, get started; commit yourself to as little as one hour per week. List the day(s) and time in the space provided.

_____

_____

_____

11 GRASPING THE PROCESS

"I am the wisest man alive for I know one thing, and that is that I know nothing."

—Socrates

JUST SHOW UP

You're dying to know the secret of successful life management; why else would you be reading this book? The truth is, the answer is at your fingertips. I once heard executive, author, and noted podcast host Seth Godin say, "Ninety-nine percent—perhaps 99.9 percent—of success happens by just showing up." Sure, Nike has its famous slogan—just do it—but I have one better: just show up. Let's look at some stories that demonstrate how it's possible to successfully work The Process by showing up.

THE BIG PICTURE

Much of what I've discussed so far entails organizing priorities to facilitate fitting more of what's important into your already-packed schedules. But there's a bigger picture to The Process. Overall, *happiness* is what we all hope to achieve. And we should be able to do more than just hope for happiness.

Each of us has the ability to be happy. But what is happiness? My idea of happiness may be different from yours, so look around—you'll easily witness many varied forms and moments of happiness. Some people always seem to be happy; others are in continual pursuit of achieving happiness. Are you one who's winning the happiness lottery or do you often come up empty handed? Stop what you're doing and reflect on this. Whether you have happiness in your life or are seeking joy, examining these moments—yours and others—will encourage your desire to make changes so that you can be happy.

At the beginning of *Exceptional Every Day*, I didn't come right out and tell you that The Process provides happiness. Instead, I wanted my description of The Process to reveal the message of happiness shining through. By analyzing and redefining priorities and then building a checklist that fits your life, I can help you get closer to daily happiness; that's where all the steps in The Process lead. Whether you call it happiness, joy, or satisfaction, I know this wonderful feeling to be The Process's natural outcome.

Happiness doesn't always come easily. Life has you down, and that is often due to many factors. Some of you are deep in the pits of despair. Even though things look bleak, you've already made incredible progress by learning with me. If you've begun to put the things we've covered into action, you're well on your way! You've shown up. You've thought about tucked-away things and asked yourself tough questions. Happiness is right here, I promise.

And if you find yourself unable to stop smiling right now, that's because you get it. The Process is already working.

PUTTING THE PIECES TOGETHER

What exactly is The Process? How do you break The Process down into its individual parts? What comes next is my version; yours may be a little different. That's okay. When I set out to write this book, I wanted to provide a foundation upon which anyone could build a plan, complete with individual meaning and a personalized version of The Process. Take what you like; discard what you don't. But whatever you do, do it with conviction. Giving up when things get a little tough or don't go your way is not an option.

This acrostic should help you remember key elements in The Process:

- **P**urpose
- **R**esults
- **O**bstacles
- **C**ulture
- **E**nthusiasm
- **S**ystems
- **S**uccess

PURPOSE

How does anything that's worth finishing begin? Everything starts with *purpose*. Purpose is the driver, the initiator, that initial spark igniting the fire. It is the *want* and the *must* and the *what*, all wrapped into one. The Process is fueled by purpose. When this lifeblood runs out, motivation falters, and regaining purpose can become quite a challenge. When you enjoy The Process and refine your plan as needed, purpose can be maintained and goals become reality.

RESULTS

Though not the be-all and end-all, results are a manifestation of The Process. Typically, "eyes on the prize" is the focus; that approach is intended to invigorate confidence and energy. Yet results are far down the line; The Process, however, is ongoing. The Process is what gets you there—results vary and change, so focusing on the outcome is pointless. That Process of continual evaluation—where you are at every step of the journey and what changes are needed along the way—will turn your work and life into something great.

OBSTACLES

You may say roadblocks, but I see stepping stones. Obstacles can be used to your advantage. Think of all the goals abandoned because of unforeseen challenges. Diet and exercise are prime examples. At first, you see solid improvement, but then bam! You plateau; weight loss and fitness gains seem to stop. Don't take this as an obstacle; think of that plateau as a challenge, one that screams, "Conquer me!" Reflect on the cause, consider options, and then step over that obstacle. Don't let the roadblocks fool you; obstacles are a vital part of growth within The Process.

CULTURE

Whether you consider it an aid or a barrier to achievements, culture surrounds you. At work, home, the gym, culture is defined by your surroundings and upbringing. The people you spend the most time with, those seated at your Table, are a direct reflection of you. Be aware. Though none of us choose the parents and family we're born into, each of us dictates who our friends are, the people we hold close. You're free to choose your culture, as it's *your* Process. So, make the most of this opportunity. You may need to make some hard decisions—and push some people from your Table—but developing your culture will be worth it.

ENTHUSIASM

Energy, smiles, a spring in the step—enthusiasm feeds your Why and makes it happy. When you feel like taking a break, enthusiasm pumps you up. It's vital to The Process; lack of enthusiasm, on the other hand, breeds bitterness and a sour aftertaste, making the work difficult to digest. Invest some enthusiasm in your Process—this natural high costs nothing and provides positive side effects. It's infectious; have you ever seen an enthusiastic person consolidate a group or bring smiles to a rough day at the office? Enthusiasm, while many things, is life's energy. Dig in and make enthusiasm your constant companion throughout The Process.

SYSTEMS

Various Processes come together through systems. This is how your Why gets your Process where it needs to go. When programmed to serve your purpose, systems are the engineering and mechanisms that adjust faults and right wrongs. Within this framework, you're able to fine-tune here and there, making larger adjustments as needed. Systems are servant leaders; they focus on the forces they're assigned to direct. Above all, systems recognize and acknowledge The Process while providing consistency and continuity. Make sure your systems serve your Process.

SUCCESS

And here we are—the finish line. This is what we hoped for, right? Hardly! What's happened at the start, in the middle, and at various checkpoints throughout your journey have meaning beyond measure. These various stations along the way are where passengers (people, ideas, ventures) are picked up or dropped off. Choices made determine not only the end results of this adventure but also the start and finish of many more journeys to come. How can an endless Process be fixated on one outcome or result? Success, then, has always been on board; your success comes with continuing to grow and achieve within your Process. And if you can simply remember that the road to success is always under construction, you will surely muster the self-motivation needed to continue building.

THE JOURNEY

In the preceding chapters, we've discussed how the end, some grand result, is not all that matters in life's journey. If that were the case, everyone would stop striving the first time we arrived at a hoped-for destination. But that one instance of success is not all we want, is it? Once we've arrived, celebrated, rested, and refueled, it's on to the next move. Much like a grand chess master who ends one game only to seek another opportunity to capture an opponent's king, we're pushing ahead, on to the next game (and then the one after that).

This is The Process in motion. This is where appreciation for the journey comes alive, where setting a purpose—defining a Why—adds to the experience. Those experiences along the way come together to form something so much greater than one result or moment of success. By aligning and refining your priorities, life becomes so much richer. The journey truly is everything.

SUCCESS STORIES

With that acrostic in mind, let's look at what I like to call "snap-shots" of a few folks I've encountered along my journey. These aren't interviews; instead, I'm depicting their lives from watching them at work and at play, from seeing times when the going gets tough or stars are aligned. I've witnessed these people at their best and at what they might contend is their worst. These descriptions are one way for me to thank a few of the friends who've shared in and helped define my Process and lent me insight into their unique jour-ney. Some snapshots are of people I don't know at all but felt an instant connection to when I heard or read their stories. If any of these inspire you, I encourage you to adopt ideas, choices, and hab-its. Make them part of your Process, too, and feel free to share; we're all in The Process of living better every day.

THE LADY ON THE RADIO

Unbelievable! It was 2017; I'd finished my early morning swim and was listening to 96.5 FM when I heard a story about an incredible woman. Amy Krouse Rosenthal had lost her life to ovarian can-cer just the week before, but her essay and podcast were recorded earlier. I listened to her describe the twenty-six beautiful years she and her husband had experienced together. They'd hoped for at least twenty-six more, but her diagnosis came just days after they'd became empty nesters; their bucket list would take a backseat to this relatively silent but very symptomatic perpetrator. She told of this new Process—what Ms. Rosenthal called "Plan B"—in her life. Time was the enemy; perspective, her ally; and so she took hold of the here and now.

Throughout the last year of her life, Ms. Rosenthal realized she wanted to do something a little unusual. Out of pure, selfless, unconditional love, she chose to write an essay about her wonderful life partner; titled "You May Want to Marry My Husband," she described how she wanted someone else to be lucky to have him. How she wanted happiness for Jason. Comfortable with her destiny, she saw no reason for her husband to suffer once she was gone.

Listening in the car, I was moved and amazed; Ms. Rosenthal embodied a godliness few can conceive, much less reach. At peace. In love. Relieved. She understood and accepted The Process and was excited to take actions she thought would help her husband *live better*. She'd learned that life could be simple once she came to grips with death. Her example is a shining one.

AARON RODGERS

If ever a professional athlete exemplified The Process, it's Aaron Rodgers. Not a sports fan? Don't have the slightest clue who Aaron is? I urge you to look him up. And don't stop reading at "NFL MVP" or "Super Bowl Champion"; dig deeper. Take a closer look.

Though Aaron had the grades and acumen to attend an Ivy League school, he wasn't highly recruited out of his Chico, California, high school. Instead, he opted to play close to home at Butte Junior College. While there, his talents caught the eyes of my friends at UC Berkeley. Soon after, he transferred there and rose to stardom. Now, having grown up in Northern California, Aaron had his sights set on playing for the beloved San Francisco 49ers. Those of us who followed the 49ers, who had the first pick in the 2005 draft, figured they'd snatch him up. But that wasn't the case. Another quarterback, Alex Smith, went to San Francisco and, as selection after selection was made, Aaron slid farther and farther from the number one pick. Though he was still the second quarterback selected in that year's draft, it wasn't until the twenty-fourth selection that Green Bay snapped Aaron up.

Though the big story was how Aaron Rodgers could've fallen that far, the young man never allowed his draft position to get to him; it was just another step in The Process. The Green Bay Packers already had future Hall of Famer Brett Favre on their roster, a player so tough he'd never missed a start. And Mr. Favre still had some good years left in his arm. Aaron didn't mind; he recognized he had an amazing opportunity to learn and absorbed every teaching moment.

In time, the back-up became the starter everyone knew he could be, rising to Super Bowl MVP (2010) and Associated Press Athlete of the Year (2011). The Associated Press also voted him the league MVP for his performance during the 2011 and 2014 NFL seasons. Not bad for someone who started out at a junior college and went twenty-fourth in the 2005 NFL draft.

As Steve Maraboli, a behavioral scientist and motivational speaker, once said, "As I look back on my life, I realize that every time I thought I was being rejected from something good, I was actually being re-directed to something better." Take a page from Aaron Rodgers' playbook; if you ever feel discouraged by a rejection, shift your perspective. See that "failure" as making space in life for even greater things to happen.

WENDY ARNOLD

She was my superior officer, so I know her as Commander Arnold, but to most she is simply Wendy. She's a fan of Wonder Woman and Marilyn Monroe, Corvette enthusiast, motorcycle-riding vixen, former U.S. Marine Corps officer, and was once the first—and lone—female combat physician serving with the U.S. Marines Special Forces. If that doesn't paint the picture of who Wendy Arnold is, nothing will.

As a family medicine physician, Wendy learned and perfected the art and skill of delivering babies; she also pursued a fellowship to master performing emergency C-sections. To boot, she knows acupuncture and can alleviate pain through hundreds of needle sticks. While deployed as Special Operations Task Force Surgeon, Wendy completed more than twenty battlefield circulations in her Humvee, supporting troops medically while covering an area close to one-third the size of Afghanistan.

Other than cool jobs and fun hobbies, what's so special about Commander Arnold? Not only does she recognize that life has everything to do with The Process but she also lives her Process every day. Whether in the clinic or at home, on the field or in her practice, Wendy always strives for *better*. I've watched with admiration as she transitions with serenity, grace, and that signature inspirational zest for life into new, challenging roles—most recently, stepmom (at age forty-four) and CEO and founder of a leadership and wellness coaching business.

Wendy never backs down from a challenge. She's passionate about self-creation and holds the conviction that life is meant to be lived. Wendy Arnold lives for The Process, believing that the adventure lies in action.

ELDRICK TONT WOODS

If any athlete in the past twenty years has suffered through the highs and lows of The Process, it's Eldrick Tont Woods. You know—Tiger Woods (what a great nickname!). Mr. Woods is often credited for irrevocably changing professional athletics; the huge sponsorships and unprecedented media attention he experienced beginning as a child athlete were phenomenal. It often seemed Mr. Woods couldn't urinate without a camera or writer attempting to witness every drop.

While most people desire money and acclaim, few would want the scrutiny and attention that accompanied Tiger Woods' every action; it would drive most of us insane. He, however, kept winning one golf tournament after another and appeared unstoppable, donning Augusta's coveted green jacket not once but *four* times (1997, 2001, 2002, and 2005). Tiger Woods was on top of the world. With his infectious smile and superior skills, success was his—everyone knew he'd keep winning and become the best professional golfer of all time.

Life, however, doesn't always follow expectations. Injuries sidelined the champion. Suddenly, Mr. Woods wasn't winning tournaments—he wasn't even making it to Sunday's final rounds. He began mixing painkillers with alcohol; he was arrested; his marriage dissolved among rumors of and confessions regarding his infidelities.

What a journey! The Process shows us that, with every great fall comes an opportunity for comeback. Tiger Woods let go of his pride and began to clean up his life. He entered therapy, got treatment, and addressed injuries—doctors did their best to clean up the bones and discs in his spine to alleviate the pain that had played such a part in his unraveling. As I write this, Mr. Woods is continuing to make a comeback and, I assume, working on his priorities. His Process is still in play.

MARK BOWERS

You know that guy—the one with a certain presence and likability many aspire to have? That's my friend, Mark Bowers. We met when I randomly chose a table at medical school orientation. I'd spent a decade in the military and it was my third day; I was older than everybody else and knew no one. So, I sat next to this guy who was beaming, like a child in a candy shop, hungry to begin. I could tell how excited he was to be there. Little did I know that this kid would become one of my best friends.

As we shook hands and made introductions, it clicked; we'd seen one another before, at 0430 in the nearby gym. Over the next four years, we'd spend many hours exercising and studying together.

On any routine day in medical school, Mark was far more dedicated than most. In our first semester, however, he received an extremely low grade in biochemistry; that didn't faze Mark. He immediately assessed the problem and made a detailed study plan (exactly what, for how long, and where to study), including daily meal preparation and free time allocation to create more time to spend on (you guessed it) studying. He also changed his daily habits, waking up earlier so he could get to the gym before class.

Mark tackled his academic problem by drawing on experience with hardship. As a teenager, he'd required surgery due to nutrient deficiency and bone loss and that had taught him a valuable lesson: there was never a reason to have an excuse. Nothing would stop him, not from becoming an orthopedic surgeon or living an active, full life.

Mark altered his Process and was off to the races. He went on to a prestigious medical center to become an orthopedic surgeon, earning a coveted spot at the famous Mayo Clinic. Mark's example teaches that enthusiastically turning obstacles, like that one small misstep in biochemistry and his past medical hardship, into stepping stones and dedicating focused energy to a plan of action will lead to success.

PROFESSOR EBEL

My friend and former professor, Ken Ebel, is more interested in personal growth—his own and others—than anyone I've ever met. Ken was one of my first college biology teachers, and he loved his students as if they were his own children. He cherished his family, held mentorship sessions on his porch, and traveled the world with his camping gear. Ken has a true zest for life.

Ken believed in me when I barely believed in myself. Teaching was about continued growth—his own, his students, and anyone he cared about. When he retired from Concordia University Irvine in 2015, he yearned for more; that passion for teaching hadn't waned.

Over the years, some ideas about ways to connect with young kids had been percolating; as a father, grandfather, and educator, Ken knew that beneficial outcomes came from early parental interest. How, then, to encourage more love and responsibility in the home? Once retired, Ken had time to ruminate on the issue and decided to mentor high school principals and help them develop the best way to reach parents and improve family responsibility. In Ken's Process, retirement created an opportunity for something new—pushing his skills to a new level and continuing personal growth.

SHAQUEM GRIFFIN

Ask me to point out one athlete who I feel follows and believes in The Process, and I'd choose Shaquem Griffin. I began following Mr. Griffin during the 2016 NCAA football season. At first glance, the University of Central Florida (UCF) Knight looked like any other starting linebacker: tall, muscular, quick, and light on his feet. He possessed an uncanny ability to get to the quarterback within seconds of the snap.

But when I looked closer, this wasn't just any college football player. Unlike other starting linebackers, Mr. Griffin has only one hand. Shaquem Griffin is a twin, and while he and his brother, Shaquill, were in their mother's womb, he developed amniotic band syndrome (strands of the amniotic sac separate and entangle digits, limbs, or other parts of the fetus, which can cause a variety of problems, depending on where strands are located and how tightly they're wrapped).

As a young child, Mr. Griffin's left hand was malformed, rounded, with small appendages projecting from its anterior surface, and never felt right. One night, his mother found him in the kitchen, holding a knife and trying to cut off his painful fingers. He was four years old. The next morning, she contacted his doctor; surgery to remove the remnants of the poorly developed hand was done that day.

Once Shaquem Griffin awoke from the anesthesia, he was immediately happy. His mother and father did not offer any sort of special treatment; they didn't want him to feel sorry for himself in any way. But that didn't mean they wouldn't be creative about helping him do the things he loved.

Both the Griffin twins loved football. As a young player, Mr. Griffin wanted to be fit and strong, just like the pros he watched on television. Nothing, not even a missing hand, was going to get in the way of his dream and, eventually, he sought a spot on a college football roster. Unlike Shaquill, who was offered scholarships from big-name college football programs (the University of Miami, University of Florida, and Florida State University), Shaquem was less sought-after. Eventually he received an offer from UCF and, since the brothers were (according to their mother) best of friends and inseparable, they signed on and headed to Orlando together.

Shaquem Griffin had a few subpar seasons at UCF. But then, he refined his skills and found his niche on the playing field. During his senior year of college, he was instrumental in leading his team to an undefeated season. And then he was invited to the NFL combine—a weeklong scouting showcase, where NFL coaches, general managers, and scouts evaluate collegiate players through a variety of physical and mental tests designed to showcase skills and facilitate draft picks.

When the 2018 NFL draft came, Shaquem Griffin made history. Drafted in the fifth round, number 141, by the Seattle Seahawks, he became the first man in the NFL with a single hand. It's unbelievable. That success can only be attributed, I believe, to his trust in The Process—Shaquem Griffin's belief in his journey was so strong that it got him exactly where he dreamed of going.

ADMIRAL KARL THOMAS

KT, as he is known to his colleagues, is a genuine leader, father, and husband. He has already surpassed a full naval career and yet he's still going. He commanded not one, but two aircraft carriers—"floating cities" of around five thousand people, more than sixty aircraft, millions of gallons of jet fuel, and perhaps a nuclear reactor or two.

The naval ship never sleeps. It cannot. There's simply too much at stake—they're prepared for impending disaster, wherever it may strike. Obviously, one man cannot run the operation all by himself. It takes a team (and a great one at that). Everyone on board has a role to follow or else safety is easily compromised. If something goes wrong, there's not much help in the middle of the big blue sea. Out of necessity, processes must be in place.

KT always embodied a "people first" mentality, which he exuded through his leadership style. You couldn't miss it. Never shy to recognize and praise in public, he offered constructive feedback behind closed doors. KT would probably say (and rightly so) that his Process was a continual work in progress, yet observers might see his career as a masterpiece. KT understood that, if values are aligned and what truly matters—relationships—is remembered, what works for one can indeed work for many.

THE HAAS FAMILY

There are those people who always show up at the right time. Of the many who've shown up in my life, Bill, Carrole, and David Haas may have been the most critical. You see, they took me in after I'd spent much of my junior and senior years of high school living in my truck.

While I was in high school, I worked for Bill and his son, David, at Sports Locker. David welcomed me into his home; thanks to moving in with him, I learned so much about a responsible home life—paying rent, sharing a bathroom, prepping my own meals, holding two jobs, playing a varsity sport—and was able to maintain a suitable grade point average for college acceptance. Having that safe, reliable, and comfortable place to stay removed a huge stressful burden from my young shoulders.

I spent dinners, holidays, and free time with Bill and Carrole, who accepted me as a second son. That acceptance was the greatest gift I'd ever received in my life. The Haas's believed in me; their love was incredible and unconditional and I felt like I was worth something. Having the Haas's as a surrogate family brought perspective to my life and awakened my Process, and I'm certain it's the heart beating in my Purpose today.

Have you ever given this sort of love to anyone? It's never too late to start and, like Bill, Carrole, and David, you may change someone's life forever.

WILLIAM L. ROBERTS

Like the Haas family, beneficial people come into my life at important times. Navy Captain (Retired) William L. Roberts became an integral part of my life just before my thirty-fifth birthday. I only wish I'd met him sooner.

William graduated from medical school the same year I was born (1979). He spent twenty-six years on active duty in the U.S. Navy and when he retired, stayed on board as a civilian physician. Our paths first crossed in 2013; I was in my fourth year of medical school, spending a month as a medical student at Camp Pendleton's Naval Hospital. William, who'd retired in 2005 and transitioned into a civilian faculty role, was in charge of that program. I still remember his firm handshake and distinguished presence—the respect he garnered from the department made an indelible impression. Before long, I sought Dr. Roberts, advice regularly.

At thirty-five, I needed lots of advice. As a younger man, I was notorious for wearing my emotions on my sleeve, letting things get to me, being unable to disguise the feelings flashing across my face. William helped me become more level-headed. He explained that being a physician meant more than leading patients; we first had to learn to lead ourselves.

Disciplined and dedicated, balance is William's forte; daily exercise, his mantra; and consistent study, his unique and defining trait. He's never accepted the easy way out nor let his budding physician students cut corners. We saw this Purpose demonstrated in his fight to beat lung cancer. *Lobectomy* is a procedure William knows quite well—though never a smoker, he's had cancerous lung tissue removed *twice*. The first time, surgeons excised two of his right lung's lobes (*bilobectomy*). Ten years later, when William's cancer returned, the third and final lobe of his right lung was amputated (removing the entire lung is a *pneumonectomy*). But having one lung hasn't beaten my mentor. Though cancer often cancels an active life, William's vibrant journey continues. The kind of consistent discipline he exhibits is quite challenging, and William's patients and colleagues benefit from witnessing his Process—put others first, find importance in everyone, and make a difference in life. William does more with one lung than most ever accomplish with two. To this day, he remains my trusted and valued mentor.

ALEX MACK

Have you met that one-of-a-kind person, an individual who inspires us beyond measure and repeatedly exceeds expectations? I have—my friend and UC Berkeley graduate school classmate, Alex Mack.

Alex has never chased personal accolades, yet I believe he's one of the NFL's best players. In college, he received the William V.

Campbell Trophy (popularly known as the "Academic Heisman"), which recognizes outstanding academics, community service, and on-field performance. Alex was drafted by the NFL in the first round; since then, he's been selected to play in the AFC-NFC Pro Bowl multiple times. His Process is that of striving to be the best he can absolutely be—not ever being satisfied, but rather continually hungry without letting the comforts he is afforded impede his progress.

Those awards might make you think Alex had it easy. He spent the first seven years of his career, however, playing for the Cleveland Browns—and they didn't have a winning record that entire time. Sure, Alex was frustrated. Like any of us, he wanted the exhilaration of winning. I thought season after losing season was frustrating—and I wasn't playing! As much as fans suffered, you'd never have known Alex was on a losing team. His frustrations were channeled into the one thing he could control: himself.

Alex worked harder and harder every day, determined he'd become the league's best teammate and center. That work ethos paid off. Teams around the league took note—Alex, they thought, would be a wise investment. His agent's phone rang and rang; eventually, multiyear contract offers started rolling in and he was rewarded with a new contract. But Alex was never about the money; he just wanted to win. When he transferred to Atlanta, Alex proved his worth by helping lead the Falcons to Super Bowl LI.

Alex displays an above-and-beyond work ethic and attitude in all facets of his life, whether he's in the books or on the field. He has a thirst for knowledge and commitment to professionalism, which is an important approach, even if you aren't a career athlete. We could all learn from Alex's Process.

DR. NIEDFELDT

During my first year of medical school, my wife was asked to speak to a group of first-year medical students about the first year caring for a baby. Believe it or not, that's how I met one of my mentors. Talk about luck and timing!

After the presentation, Danika came home and told me about this doctor who'd interviewed her. The man, Dr. Mark Niedfeldt, was one of the medical school's volunteer professors; I found out he was also a team doctor for the Milwaukee Brewers. A week later, in anatomy class, I met him. We talked about running and "toe shoes" (you've seen them; they look like gloves for your feet. They're a type of minimalist footwear originally developed and marketed as a more natural shoe for kayaking and sailing that gained alternative popularity with runners and hikers); Mark and I were testing the shoes during our workouts—on a side note, I've been wearing Vibram FiveFingers for ten years now.

Mark invited me to tour his medical practice and then catch a Milwaukee Brewers baseball game so I could see his passion for sports medicine in action. I've always been interested in the field, so this was the beginning of my mentorship (though I'm not sure how Mark fit another thing into his busy schedule). He had his own private practice and worked night shifts in an orthopedic hospital. Did I mention the 162-game baseball season? Because he shared the Brewers job with two other doctors, he didn't have to go to every single game, but still—that's a lot of baseball. Eventually, he became a team physician for the Milwaukee Bucks, U.S. National Snowboarding and Freeskiing Teams, and Milwaukee Ballet. And as a devoted father of three, I'm not sure he ever slept.

And despite all those obligations, Mark still found time to guide me through the field of sports medicine. He even attended my medical school graduation ceremony and the intimate celebration following at our home. This, I thought, was proof that you can never be too busy to touch a life; when you know your limitations and priorities and make sure The Process aligns with your goals, all things are possible. If not for the giving example set by Mark and other people like him, most of us would never understand the importance of investing our time in others. Mark's generosity made it easy for me to comprehend this lesson and then pay it forward.

SEÑORA DE HUBER

I couldn't write about success stories without including my amazing high school Spanish teacher, Señora de Huber. I believe she knows the impact she has had on me. We've remained in contact because her never-ending pursuit to learn more and her dedication to wringing the most out of each day continue to inspire me. Though in her nineties, Señora de Huber is still traveling the globe, visiting family and appreciating the world.

Señora de Huber possesses a pizazz, a "never stop living" ethos, that's centered around The Process. Through her example, I've learned that, if you love what you do and maintain a zest for life, you cannot help but happily *live better*.

ADAM MCLINTOCK

My first roommate on a "floating city" (the aircraft carrier also known as CVN76 and the USS *Ronald Reagan*) was Adam McLintock. Both of us still wet behind the ears, just out of flight school, we checked into that first fleet squadron together. Adam started at the very bottom of the Navy's food chain (as an enlisted man, painting and cleaning ships) but progressed to win a military scholarship to prestigious Vanderbilt University and earn an officer commission, which led to flying on and off aircraft carriers with me.

Though only five feet seven inches tall, Adam's wonderfully

magnetic personality made him stand out in any group. Kind, loquacious, and committed, he was the kind of friend everyone wants. We were yin to the other's yang; Adam sought my advice on diet and exercise while I turned to him on social matters. The product of divorce, Adam was essentially an only child, his two older half-sisters busy with their own lives, and so he missed out on a lot of childhood nurturing. Perhaps that's why he possessed such a desire to make connections; Adam truly enjoyed spending time in people's company and could find a way into any conversation.

After three years in a sea-going combat-ready squadron, deployed around the globe, Adam headed to Washington DC's political arena, continuing his travels (even sneaking across the Israeli border to catch Metallica, his favorite band, in concert). Though long stretches of radio silence fell between visits and phone conversations, Adam and I could always pick up where we left off.

Though he couldn't readily put his finger on exactly how, Adam wanted to make a difference. Jumping from one job to another, it seemed for brief times as if Adam had lost sight of his Process (we all do). But he was really letting The Process play out. You see, Adam truly enjoys the journey and is open to possibilities; he's never possessed a "right way or the highway" attitude. From enlisted man to whatever lies ahead, Adam's Process has always meant more than any destination.

COACH AURIEMMA

Here's someone who truly enjoys The Process. Coach Geno Auriemma's job, passion, and life revolve around coaching women's basketball at the University of Connecticut (UConn). He has won more games and championships than nearly any coach who's ever stepped onto the hardwood. As I write this, Coach Auriemma's preparing his team for yet another shot at the NCAA Women's Basketball

Championship (win three more games, and they'll hold the trophy a twelfth time and score another undefeated season). What he's accomplished with UConn is unheard of in the sport. And yet, because they've won so often, many basketball fans despise the Huskies. Why? They'd love to see someone new win the title.[7]

UConn does lose, though. In 2017, they had a good run but came up short of the title. Throughout that imperfect season, however, Coach Auriemma never lost sight of The Process: in the bigger game of life, losing is at the heart of winning. He's taught his players to truly believe in the art of The Process, showing them throughout the years that they can enjoy the game without obsessing over the results. I don't know anyone in sports or life who's done a better job of teaching The Process and showing others how it should be done.

MY BEST FRIEND

She can make anyone smile. Even though her name is often incorrectly pronounced, I've never heard her correct anyone. She's an unassuming, humble person, someone who's likely to say "I'm sorry" when she's not at fault, so she's upset I've mentioned her here. Of course, *Exceptional Every Day* wouldn't be complete without her.

The woman I am speaking of is my wife, Danika—pronounced *duh-NEE-ka*. Her unwavering support and sacrifice got me through battles with cancer, close calls, medical school's rigors, and life's ups and downs. Whether it's her degenerative elbow or that unassuming nature again, Danika is unable to pat herself on the back, even though she deserves it. So, I will. She loves to please others, even when they're far from deserving.

Though caring for our family occupied her and obscured her

---

7   Unfortunately for Geno and his players, UConn lost 2018's final championship game. Congratulations, Notre Dame.

Process, once Danika found that daily persistence was her focus, she was on a roll. As an adolescent, she'd been stuck with a debilitating disease. She didn't, however, make excuses; she didn't ever want to suffer through "being sick." Danika wanted to live fully: exercise, travel, help and please others, and be the best mother possible. Rather than settle for pills or a weekly injection, she viewed food and exercise as prescriptions to manage her degenerative disease. While Danika hasn't won every fight, she will tell you she's always very happy she's tried. Her Process revolves around accepting life as it is, refraining from excuses, and taking—and recovering from—life's punches, one round at a time.

FINDING A HEALTHY FINALE

The end. Finale. The point in the game when the clock strikes zero, the buzzer sounds, and one team walks away, loathing the agony of defeat, while the other basks in the glory of victory. Done. Process complete, Why realized, Purpose fulfilled. After all, our journey through life is solely about those end results, right?

Wrong!

I call this type of thinking *destination addiction*. While having the end in mind is a very healthy and valuable way to start any endeavor, it shouldn't be your sole focus. That's too much pressure to place upon yourself. Destination addiction will push you to overindulge, obsess, and create a poor outcome. How do I know? I've been there, done that.

During 2011, I attended the Summer Institute for Medical Students (SIMS) program at the Betty Ford Center in Palm Springs, California. This center is home to one of the nation's most renowned drug and alcohol rehabilitation programs. By no means cheap, participation in the program is biased toward those who are financially secure; I was neither wealthy nor alcoholic but, thanks to the amazing philanthropy and annual sponsorship of Tom and Maripat Dalum, longtime supporters of the Medical College of Wisconsin, I was able to leave my family and devote myself to studying and learning about alcohol addiction at the center.

That summer, I became immersed in studying a ruthless disease that destroys the mind and the body. (If you're one of those people who refuses to consider alcoholism a disease, I challenge you to learn about it; there are reams of research.) I spent hours studying in a classroom and in one-on-one sessions with patients, where I met spouses, children, and other family members who'd become emotionally exhausted from alcoholism's effects, many of whom had completely lost hope. All those failed attempts, dashed hopes about this recovery, and relapses left them skeptical. For many, however, a few days of instruction and self-learning renewed possibilities of hope for their loved ones. An eager student, I absorbed all of it. The long days never seemed boring or wasteful, especially as my own demons came to life.

Whereas my addictions had nothing to do with drugs or alcohol (I was too scared to even drink a glass of wine), I've always been overly ambitious regarding exercise and work. I often went to extremes, chasing results, and thinking *more* is better. That destination thinking nearly destroyed me; poor outcomes typically surround any type of addiction. For example, too much exercise or dietary restriction is not a good thing. I've experienced many lonely moments of self-destructive activity, even though some might consider the addiction "positive." Perhaps you've been there, too.

Maintaining a healthy balance—focusing on the here-and-now, staying on track with your goals, and enjoying the moment—is key to combatting destination addiction. Life goes by way too fast, and it goes by even faster when you don't see the big picture. Now, I'm not saying forget about where you want to end up; that would be a horrible mission objective and lead to minimal success. But if all you're doing is looking at the destination, you'll surely miss beautiful sights, beautiful rest stops, and life-changing, diversionary adventures along your Process. Life's roadmap isn't a straight line (though easy, straightforward lines can be quite addicting), and attempting to live without a single course adjustment is like being a gymnast who's so focused on the balance beam she never takes in the rest of the competition.

Enjoying The Process means each of us must be willing to notice and participate in life's detours and accept the ride's accompanying terrain, those highs and lows. I know embracing here-and-now is not easy; if it were, I'd have no reason to write this book. Success, however, requires you let go of the single-minded pursuit of results and, when you grasp this part of The Process, appears at the doorstep. Even when you don't expect it, success will know and find you. With destination addiction a thing of the past, nothing can hold you back from all the wonderful experiences that lie ahead.

ENJOYING THE PROCESS

Denis Waitley, the motivational speaker behind "Winning for Life," said, "It is not in the pursuit of happiness that we find fulfillment, it is in the happiness of the pursuit." As we've discussed The Process, I've thrown an array of ideals your way; even though I've tried to refrain from "too much too fast" and creating sensory overload, we've discussed many thoughtful topics. And now that it's time to reflect, you may feel overwhelmed.

I get it. Challenging long-held beliefs can seem like all work and no play. But The Process is supposed to be fun, not a joyless slog. I never said The Process would be simple. Things that matter most—such as personal growth, coalescing work and passion—take time, nurturing, and continued attention. Answering questions and reflecting at the end of each chapter help you see the joy experienced from taking a deep dive into your life's story. Establishing and rewriting priorities, thinking about how to do things better, eliminating waste in your life, and searching for *more* are bringing you closer to success with every day. Truth is, you're having fun—though you might not know it just yet. Remember: this Process involves realizing self-awareness and you are only now arriving.

Do me a favor—pause right now. Put down your book (whether print, digital, or audio) and, for a few minutes, do something purely for yourself. It can be anything that brings joy (walking your dog, playing with the kids, reading a favorite book, giving an old friend a call to simply check in). Whatever you choose, that joy is part of your Process, and it won't end here.

When you come back, I look forward to our next shared adventure. There's still a little more to do before I set you completely free on your Process.

END-OF-CHAPTER ASSESSMENT

Has this chapter helped you gain a better appreciation for what The Process really is? I'm hoping that these stories have illustrated that The Process is *you*. Everything you do is rolled into this singular vehicle for getting where you want to go. Between that handy acrostic and stories about intentional people—from professional athletes to everyday people—I've shared tools for successfully working your Process. And rather than focus on results, I've encouraged you to enjoy The Process and reminded you to savor each moment of life's continuous ebb and flow.

Questions for Reflection and Direction

What you see here is the entire Process Checklist, which summarizes each priority covered in *Exceptional Every Day*. Before moving on to the next chapter, take a moment to review each checklist and answer the questions that follow in the spaces provided or your own journal. When you're ready, I'll meet you in Chapter 12.

THE PROCESS CHECKLIST

Priority 1—You

Priority 2—Your Why

Priority 3—Your One Thing

Priority 4—Your Daily Table

Priority 5—Your Work and Passion

Priority 6—Your Family and Friends

Priority 7—Your Mind and Body

Priority 8—Spirituality and the Soul

Priority 9—Rest, Play, and Sleep

Priority 10—Something Bigger Than You

1. Using the Process Checklist, write your priority list. Be sure to keep the fundamentals in mind as you go.

_____

_____

_____

2. Now that you've listed your priorities, organize them by creating a Process Map. Your Process Map is a visual way of looking at your life and priorities. (This is an initial outline, so don't worry about making it perfect; you'll be refining it in the next chapter.)

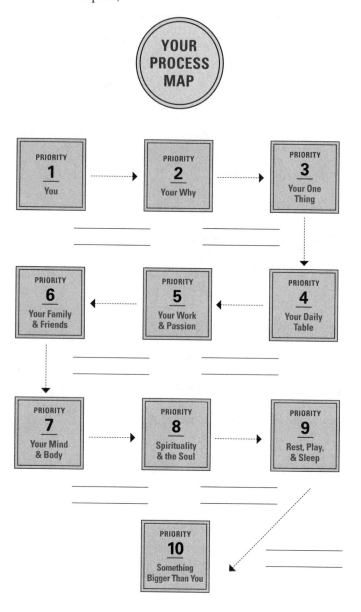

3. The Process is only good if it is used. How do you plan to get started? You'll likely need more space than I've provided here, so feel free to write your Process plan in a journal.

_____

_____

_____

12 TAKING YOUR TURN

"See the world as it is. Be the boss of you."
—Seth Godin

Time is not a renewable resource. This hour that lies ahead is finite—3,600 seconds in length—and now you have only 2,997 remaining. As those seconds tick by, I thank you for sticking around for this long. Having made it this far (assuming you haven't skipped too many pages and you're not a world-class speed reader), you've invested a great deal of time. Along the way, you've built confidence around managing your life; as you've created and fostered relationships, you've begun to learn and grow. Now it's time to take the next steps, grab control of those future seconds, and make your Process count.

REFINING YOUR PROCESS

There's something very special about new beginnings. It's very plausible that before picking up *Exceptional Every Day*, you'd never analyzed your life as a *process*. Now that you have, I doubt you'll ever stop finding your own unique interpretations and applications. Because The Process is different for everyone, I've outlined broad steps to help you successfully manage your life. Use this template to fill in the blanks and expand and refine your thinking—and, most importantly, *live it out*.

It's your turn to review your life! Start with a simple checklist. Mind you, a checklist is radically different from a to-do list. A to-do list is restrictive; it tells what you *must* do—which hardly allows room to grow. A checklist, on the other hand, guides toward desirable paths, or what you *want* to do; it keeps us focused, in a loving spirit, and allows for alterations. It should propel you toward the life you've always dreamed of, an abundant, limitless life, full of relationships, significance, and ultimately fulfillment. Sure, that can include making more money or driving a nicer car. But anything worth doing must include an initial question or proposal for the beginning to keep going in a meaningful way. Every Process requires a Why.

To take your turn and begin this new journey, I need to make sure you're equipped and ready with a proper set of values and appropriate priorities. Your grand entrance relies more on your ability to adapt and learn than on past lessons. While experience will help guide you, constant and deliberate desire will enable you to find better, more effective methods to propel you forward.

BEGIN WITH THE END IN MIND

Stephen Covey's world-renowned book, *The 7 Habits of Highly Effective People,* points toward "beginning with the end in mind."

When you think about where you want to go, odds of getting there are much greater; along the way, you will make conscious decisions instead of sitting around waiting for life to happen. Remember The Process Map you developed, that initial outline based on specific priorities, tailored to fit your life? Just like Goldilocks, that "just right" fit is crucial: too baggy (everyone can do without extra problems in life) or too tight (no one wants to feel restricted, unable to move and grow) will mean lack of balance and constant life adjustments—and that won't cut it.

Successful life management means accounting for those twenty-four hours—all 86,400 seconds—in each day. You're the only one who can define being *you,* and The Process is ready to help with every step in the journey toward becoming your best and most valuable *you.*

BUILDING YOURSELF, DAY BY DAY

When we talk about library books, "renew" means keeping the same book a little bit longer. But within The Process, we use *renew* in terms of inventing, invigorating, freshening, nourishing, and assessing *yourself* again—a form of continual, daily pursuit. Committing to The Process isn't a one-off, like trying a new juice cleanse or going on a seven-day fast. It's persistently committing to self-improvement because you know it's the right way, not some fad that fades away.

Are you willing to become uncomfortable with being average? Your self-worth is a direct reflection of choices made; those decisions determine how far and exactly where you'll go in life. The Process provides all the tools needed; now, you're figuring out how to access your inner toolbox. Though unlocked, that toolbox may feel inaccessible—maybe it's rusty, you've lost the key, or the lock is broken. That's nothing to fret over; you'll get the access you need, when you need it. By committing to The Process, you've cracked the lid (unlike folks who've failed to find their toolbox or even have an interest in picking them up at all).

Remember that having tools isn't enough; you must use them right to see results. Start building by working every day. No carpenter or artist creates a single piece of furniture, home, or beautiful piece of artwork right away. They practice their craft throughout their lives. The Process is no different. Finishing this book doesn't mean you're done; there's so much more to building yourself. The priorities revealed and discussed throughout *Exceptional Every Day* are meant for life's long haul. You don't analyze or reevaluate and then put that priority away; you analyze and acknowledge deficits and then get to work. Like that master woodworker, you learn to build something beautiful step by step, day by day.

TAKE TIME OUT TO REFLECT

Building beauty in life can only occur through self-examination and reflection—where you are in life, how you got there, what has caused failures, how you've recovered, who has influenced you, and so on. Not practicing self-examination? Why not?

Daily self-examination doesn't take big chunks of time. It's rather like taking a quick snapshot or selfie. Sometimes, getting enough distance in the middle of events while they're happening is difficult, so examine your interactions afterward.

After a conversation, meal with a friend, workout at the gym, or that brief interaction with the clerk at the grocery store, quickly and efficiently think about what just happened. Register what you did well (so you can do it again) and what could've gone better (for growth). Without practicing self-reflection, no real improvement to your Process can occur; only by peeling back the layers and discovering who's inside (beyond the superficial self, the *you* others see walking down the street or entering a room) can real growth occur.

Simply acknowledging wrongs—bad habits and choices; all those times you weren't paying attention—and accepting what needs to be done better next time will create a new perspective, foster growth, and allow your best self to shine. Remember that unconditional love for yourself is an important part of The Process. Nothing's worse than a coach who only finds fault, so don't be too hard on yourself. Self-reflection also means thanking yourself for what went right.

While you're at it, reflect on this: you are innately valuable just for being you. Created exactly as you should be, no shiny new car, added degree, award, or number of Twitter followers will increase your human worth. Instead of focusing on acquiring things, ask yourself: Have I gone the extra mile for the rest of the world? Did I treat myself—and others—well today? If you don't like the answers, The Process can help find ways to change and move forward in your journey of personal growth.

THE NEED FOR CONSTANT EVALUATION

As we've learned, The Process never stops. If we want to improve, then we must always evaluate ourselves. During my third year of medical school, I shared lockers during surgical rotations with my friend Jared Forrester, who'd played college football. (You may recall that it was Jared who comforted me the day I learned my baby daughter, Siena, had hearing loss.) Inside our locker, he posted this quote: "Every day, you're either getting better or getting worse, because nothing ever stays the same."

As I'd don my scrubs for what was surely to be another fourteen hours (or more) on the ward and in the operating room, I'd recite that quote. And I thanked Jared for sharing it, because being pulled in so many different directions—going from one operating room to the next, surgery after surgery, all those long hours—made it easy to lose sight of myself. Because I was never able to fully appreciate any procedure's result, I'd often wonder, *How did the patient do after leaving the hospital?* That lack of closure was unrewarding; while surgeons can often instantly "fix" their patients, I wanted to become a family medicine doctor—though getting results may take weeks, months, and sometimes, even years. I've found that getting someone to make lifestyle changes is the ultimate panacea.

The problem, however, is lifestyle changes cannot be purchased via infomercial. Unlike making one or two easy payments of $39.95, there's no money-back guarantee. They are, however, worth the investment; beneficial lifestyle choices may enable you to take a dream trip, see your grandchildren grow up, and chip away at that bucket list, one amazing adventure at a time. Solutions to health problems (and living a better life) aren't quick fixes; they take work and lots of consistent self-evaluation, part of a difficult Process that involves time and effort—this isn't about instant gratification. (Sure, some health changes—quitting smoking, for example—actually do lead to instantaneous improvement and some positive effects are noticeable right away, but that's an exception.) Knowing where you stand means you can better dictate where you wish to go. So, practice self-reflection. Streamline your Process. Grow and get better. Smooth out bumps and press on with being a better *you*.

SACRIFICE

Considering modern technology and a world that thrives on instantaneous gratification, I wonder—has sacrifice lost its luster? I've always felt that giving up something important to me to help someone else was rather easy. Maybe that's because I was introduced to the concept at a young age, but I don't believe my childhood is the entire answer. An ability to sacrifice develops from myriad experience and reveals itself in various forms. Sacrifice keeps us yearning toward goals and aligns our journey; it redefines priorities and, ultimately, our Process. In fact, I feel *sacrifice* and *process* could be used almost interchangeably.

Seth Godin, one of my mentors (and the man whose words open this chapter), helps paint this picture of an almost synonymous relationship between the two terms. "Sacrificing," he wrote, "might mean giving up an expenditure, but it can also be the bold step of having a difficult conversation now instead of later. Regardless of the goal, sacrifice makes it more likely that you will get there. We are never certain that we will reach our goal, one significant reason that so few people persist. But if the journey involves sacrifice, we're paying for that goal, the goal we're never sure to reach, every day."[8]

SAY GOODBYE TO DISTRACTIONS

If you didn't pick up on this concept thus far, I'll restate it now: You *must* remove distractions to successfully manage life. The more distractions are eliminated, the more time you'll gain for what matters. Distractions pull us off course. They are selfish, seeking only to feed themselves, and lack empathy.

Hold on, you say; *what about my children? They're certainly a distraction in pursuing work and other outside-the-home goals, but labeling them this way is rude and ignorant.* Aha! You, my intelligent friend, have answered your own question. Your children are not the same kind of distraction that, say, email and talk radio can be. We're differentiating between the many time-sucks that plague your day and those precious beings seated at your daily Table (and if they aren't, they should be). What's important is recognizing how time with family adds, not diverts, worth to life's journey.

Perhaps you grew up as one of those children whose parents viewed family as a negative distraction. How do you feel about that

---

8   http://sethgodin.typepad.com/seths_blog/2018/03/delighting-in-sacrifice.html.

today? Not a good feeling, is it? Part of The Process is examining past hurts and regrets to make sure we don't perpetuate them and visit them upon others.

Distractions abound. They pull at and undermine our priorities every day. Sooner or later, there's no choice but to return to what matters—our priorities—and the longer you wait, the more painful that self-reflection becomes (perhaps, as you read this, you're chuckling—you know it's true). And it's to your advantage to not keep your Process waiting.

ALLOCATING YOUR ENERGY

Look a little deeper into this talk about managing precious seconds and your life and you'll see that it essentially comes down to energy. Doing anything requires energy. You accumulate energy by understanding abilities; you build systems and your Process—you manage time—by fueling your body with proper exercise, food, and rest; by examining priorities with a keen sense of awareness; by looking at your life through the correct lens. Some, however, argue that trying to manage time is impossible, but I beg to differ.

Though they were going after a niche market, Ken Blanchard and Spencer Johnson, authors of *The One Minute Manager*, saw the light at the end of this tunnel. Their work parallels my thoughts; by properly allocating and efficiently addressing energy devoted to tasks and to-do lists, you are truly managing time. Breaking the task into small, achievable segments—managing one minute of the day at a time rather than tackling the entire twenty-four hours—is no different than putting one part of life—spirituality, your job, a ten-year plan, for example—into perspective versus the entire future.

Take sitting in a dry sauna after a morning workout. I'm here because Tim Ferriss, author of *The 4-Hour Workweek*, persuaded me that doing so can increase growth hormone release. So, I've allocated fifteen to twenty minutes before work to do this. A few of those minutes are for meditation or mindfulness; the rest for journaling and reading (the sauna is a surprisingly perfect place for these activities).

Today, while I'm meditating, a guy is making weird noises; another is playing video games on his iPad. While I can only control my own use, boy, do I want to share my secrets about mindfully allocating energy with these guys!

THE PROCESS MINDSET

Think about those guys in the sauna. Every path taken leads to another choice, and some of those choices have the power to change everything. The rest of your life hangs on those choices and how much time and energy we'll need to do the things that matter. It's simple: fulfilling your Process comes down to focus.

Where, then, are your choices focused? Please don't tell me your critical life moments revolve around fleeting, material possessions. Luxury goods will only last so long and get you so far. Life's journey—the adventure and experience we know as The Process—will always be more meaningful than shiny baubles. The exhilaration of *doing* will always trump that of *having*, and that requires a special mindset—of appreciation and flexibility, enough to move obstacles; a willingness to try new things and learn; desire to function outside the box and live life to its fullest. When your mindset becomes the Way, you can better see what lies ahead and make focused choices at meaningful forks in life's road.

CULTIVATING MINDFULNESS

At the core of Zen Buddhism's teachings is a clear mind or, more appropriately, a "beginner's mind." This mindset can move mountains and bring a sense of freedom, but such clarity takes work. Clearing and disciplining thoughts to focus on one thing at a time is something to strive for, and mindfulness within The Process can only come with training and an understanding of the rules of the road. Success in chosen endeavors will necessitate course corrections, as uncontrollable forces will result in drift. If we lack mindfulness, true potential may remain persistently on the horizon.

I'm not saying that success requires mindfulness. Just look around and you'll see this is hardly the case. Plenty of successful people in an array of areas—from TV to your workplace—appear to be anything but mindful and clear in thought. You and I, however, want more.

To achieve mindfulness and live with energy, you need only to be free. Allow quiet time; be willing to put away electronics (for just a few minutes); steer clear of negative people and thoughts. If you can do these things for a few minutes day after day, you pave the way for a new mental arena.

Once you've harnessed the ability to think clearly and without clutter, life will fall into place and your inner superhero will be unleashed. You won't dream or wish for The Process—you'll own your own. Do not disregard the power behind this paradigm shift but continue to develop it.

PUTTING PROCESS TO WORK

Have you seen stickers on cars displaying numbers? Generally, these refer to the number of miles someone inside the vehicle has run, biked, swum, or raced. While I've done my fair share of these, I don't feel mileage is an accomplishment I must share; whether others know isn't important to me. If you have a sticker like this, I don't mean to sound critical (especially after you've invested so much time validating my thoughts by reading this book). The truth is, no one needs to know because you don't need their validation. Others, though, have bought into a culture of reputation.

Reputation is what other people think you are. I believe, however, that *character* is what matters. Character is who you are when no one else is there to see; character needs no sticker. In life's grand race, there is no entry fee to gain acceptance, no cut-off time to meet, no medal at the end. Life's grand race begins the day you're born and doesn't end until your heart stops beating and you draw that last breath. You don't participate for the audience. If you like the mileage sticker, fine; keep a tally, but don't center your life around that number. Do 13.1, 26.2, and 140.6 because you want to enjoy the course, not to prove your worth.

IT'S YOUR TURN

This segment is about claiming *your* priorities and living *your* fullest life. If I were to make a sticker for this philosophy, it would surely read: "I'm still running. How about you?"

I'm not sure I was ever meant to be physician (or a millionaire, professional athlete, or any number of professions), but I am sure of my purpose, my Why—adding value to others' lives. Gaining that "MD" is a means to an end, granting me access and ability to help people. My chosen profession has tested my philosophies about life, motivation, and inspiration (and anything else that might result from being with a patient or participating in a group seminar). Choosing medical school, family medicine, and now sports medicine tested my Process on every level.

My life is not perfect; I've failed many times; I will continue to strive and succeed and fail until that final breath. The Process, however, saves me. And I'd like you to find that same comfort in your Process. Think about your Why—and if you don't know your Why at this moment, that's totally okay. Finding mine took a long time;

that journey is one of the reasons I wrote *Exceptional Every Day*. But don't wait to uncover and define your purpose; the clock is ticking and you must get going. The Process does not stop or take breaks but is constantly in motion—each of us is growing, shedding, and redefining continually and consistently.

As you look at life and all the parts involved in your Processes, do you see where the big picture and these priorities intersect and intertwine? Ask yourself some questions: *What can I do better? What does life hold in store; what are my expectations? Can I exceed those anticipated limits and become more?* Oh, there's an infinite number of questions you may want to ask, just as there is no limit to growth or beauty within your Process. By putting your Process in motion and mindfully cultivating your choices each day, your life will be a true success.

LEAVING YOUR LEGACY

Every step in your journey, good and bad, creates a personal legacy. My mentor and friend, John Maxwell, has said that "lasting value is measured by succession." How someone follows, when it's our turn to plan for tomorrow (and everyone eventually leads and manages life with another day in mind), legacy—what we leave behind—takes many forms. How that looks only you can determine.

An intentional Process helps create the legacy you desire. Whether you're fifty-five, thirty-seven, or eighteen years old, everyone must consider the same thing first: What are you willing to give up?

Through the course of this book, you've determined essential priorities and developed a sense of *what matters most to you*. You've created and edited a personal checklist and are prepared for what life may toss your way. Once you know what you can do without, the things you're willing to give away—be they time, money, opportunities, a certain lifestyle—you can take initiative and start The Process.

You see, no matter where you turn or look, The Process is waiting. Because it is a part of you, The Process cannot abandon you. Because The Process does not act on its own behalf or quit when times are tough, it will never set you up for failure.

The Process is dynamic, so once your Process Map is in place, you must remain focused. Your goals don't have to be static—change, after all, is a good thing—but they must be known. And in order to reach new goals (remember, The Process is never about just one goal but a lifetime of goals), you must possess determination and the desire to share. That succession, passing on what you've created to those who come after, can be theory (ideas that, one day, are assimilated into their life) or actual, a direct handoff. Either way, realizing your Process should produce the legacy you desire—and deserve—to leave behind.

* * *

Me and some fifty people—parents, children, friends—are about to watch my girls perform in their first music recital at the Museum of Making Music in Carlsbad, California. Elle and Siena took up music lessons about six months ago—one with the piano, the other on the violin—and their duet will last a very short amount of time (though I'm sure these are seconds our family will never forget). They've spent months preparing for less than one minute of execution.

From hours of practice with their teacher, Hector, to broken strings and out-of-tune instruments, their Process has its own variations. Seeing the fruits of my girls' music lessons, something my parents lacked awareness of, much less funds for, (and I likely lack ability to do—you don't want to hear me sing) brings a smile to my face.

I know how easy it is to get caught up in doing: writing one more page, checking off another box. Like any busy person, I've often allowed a hectic schedule to intrude on life's joy and make happiness suffer. But not today. For this special occasion, I put aside my comfortable clothes to dress up; today's recital brings a sense of renewal and relief. Today, I am happy—happy to see my journey is reflected in my children. Because of my life, my daughters live and experience life, and so I share this simple story to show The Process's profound impact through succession.

END-OF-CHAPTER ASSESSMENT

From making refinements to constantly reflecting and evaluating priorities and goals, life's journey progresses ever forward. In this chapter, we've examined mindset and how eliminating distractions that clutter your path are key to a flourishing Process. You already possess the necessary tools—I've merely shown you the toolbox; now, it's your turn to get to work. You're set to make a huge impact on your life and the lives of others.

Questions for Reflection and Direction

Before moving on to the next chapter, take a moment to answer the following questions in the space provided or your own journal. When you're ready, I'll meet you in the Conclusion.

YOUR PROCESS MAP

1. Reference the Process Map created in the previous chapter. Do you need to make changes? If so, revise your Process Map in the space provided.

YOUR PROCESS MAP
PRIORITY 1 You
PRIORITY 2 Your Why
PRIORITY 3 Your One Thing
PRIORITY 4 Your Daily Table
PRIORITY 5 Your Work & Passion
PRIORITY 6 Your Family & Friends
PRIORITY 7 Your Mind & Body
PRIORITY 8 Spirituality & the Soul
PRIORITY 9 Rest, Play, & Sleep
PRIORITY 10 Something Bigger Than You

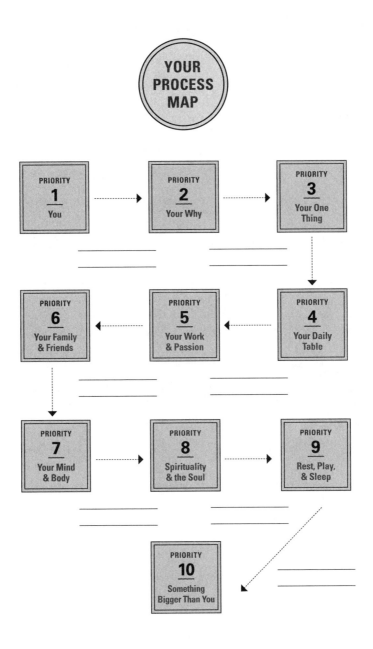

2. Consider your goals. What are things you'd like to accomplish in the next three days? Two weeks? Six months? Three years?

_____

_____

_____

3. Imagine sharing your Process with those at your Table so they can better understand you. How would you tell them about it? (Remember: you can only teach if you actually know.)

_____

_____

_____

4. Congratulations! Managing your life just became a reality. What do you plan on doing now?

_____

_____

_____

CONCLUSION

"If one advances confidently in the direction of his dreams, and endeavors to live the life which he has imagined, he will meet with a success unexpected in common hours."

—Henry David Thoreau

My friend Greg, a twenty-year Marine Corps veteran, told me he hates the word "process." He says it sounds too structured and machine-like (and this coming from a man who yelled at recruits for a living—and enjoyed it!). I see his point; *process* is a rather straightforward concept with a succinct definition. Yet, it can be so much more complex.

No two readers are alike, and I hope to have conveyed my purpose in various ways, under various lights, through examples of The Process at work (and there are endless examples, as we all are unique). If The Process were a one-size-fits-all wardrobe, there'd be no excitement or challenge in opening its doors.

Remember that The Process only feels restricting if you allow it. There's continual change; you're always working and finding ways to get better, do more, and release enthusiasm. The Process yearns for freedom and, if it could talk, it would say *let the river flow. Don't dam life up. Give a little more to get more out of yourself.* The power of The Process is that *more* is always possible.

What does it mean to "manage" your time? Well, we're always going to want more; many of us want more than 86,400 seconds. After all, you'd get more done in, say, a twenty-eight-hour day. But the truth is, the amount of time we already have is perfect. We just need to prioritize what we fill our day with. The Process proves that *not enough time* does not equal not enough *life.*

The Process—our journey, path, trail through life—isn't a free-way. Chances are, there will be detours, caution signs, one-way exits and entry points, and an array of unexpected delays. An attitude that recognizes life's delays as part of personal growth and develop-ment creates an environment where The Process thrives.

PERSONAL SUCCESS

My mentors have led me to almost daily reflection on and renewal of my purpose. The amount of time varies; some days, I spend just a few seconds or minutes; on others, I look deeply and profoundly into the things that make me tick. This practice has fulfilled me through building my definition of personal success. Fulfilled, but only slightly satisfied, because there is so much more to do.

How do I define personal success? Many components deserve credit, but this book provides something simple and easy to imple-ment. I wanted to provide concepts you could quickly absorb and immediately integrate into your life. I've provided some tools—the daily Table, Process Checklist, and Process Map—for you to use and adjust as needed. I've also included templates for these tools in the Appendices, because The Process is ever-changing.

THE PROCESS IN THREE SIMPLE CONCEPTS

We're all pressed for time, so let's review by condensing the ten Process priorities. The resulting three simple concepts can be quickly and efficiently reflected on when you're busy. If I could revisit my eighteen-year-old self, I'd start him on a daily reflection habit with these simple Priorities:

1. Know your purpose.

2. Grow to your maximum potential.

3. Sow seeds to benefit others.

Why these three? First, only by fully understanding and believing in Why can you move mountains. When you know your purpose, there's no wasted time wandering and drifting off course. By discovering your Why, anything is possible and managing your life will feel like a choice, not a burden.

Second, planting a garden today will produce fruits that feed you for the rest of your life. Daily growth—that focus on becoming a better person—allows you to stretch and expand and become *more*.

And third, finding your benefit to others enables *significance*. We leave our mark on the future by functioning as a significant vehicle in other people's lives. Self-reflection reveals how these efforts are realized and enjoyed.

When you're pressed for time, remember these three concepts. Quick, mindful reflection will put you on a clear path to success.

AFTERWORD

As an aviator, I was taught to keep my head on a swivel and an eye on my surroundings. I was sold on the notion that a flinch or mis-step could mean compromise, injury, or death. Talk about stress! No wonder so many military folks suffer from anxiety, depression, insomnia, and post-traumatic stress disorder—what I call "sensory overload in its finest hour."

So, what does that sensory overload have to do with *you*? Abso-lutely everything. Life is full of distractions that mean little or nothing. It's easy to get caught up in trivialities, lose sight of vision and purpose, and bog down in interference, static, and noise. Like a viscous mud, those things stick in all the wrong places. It's impos-sible to wash off, exfoliate, burn, or run away—the crud keeps on giving. That is, if you let those toxic distractions settle within you in the first place.

Getting a handle on sensory overload requires managing those things that you can control. The Process teaches focusing on thoughts and your personal Why; don't waste time on all the other things you can't control. Go and conquer the life you've been gifted (yes, you read that correctly). Whether you view yourself as a child of God or product of evolution (or both), be grateful for having breath to take and life to manage. You have an opportunity and challenge to discover and build your perspective and create a meaningful legacy.

Remember, my friends, life is *all* about The Process. I challenge you to take hold of each day's 86,400 seconds—though they may sometimes feel like community property, they are yours alone. When you claim your time, you'll become happier and more fulfilled; with every breath you take, you'll experience a rewarding feeling of success. For better (and worse), The Process keeps churning; its wheels rolling through rain, sleet, and snow and rocking with the thrill of victory and the agony of defeat. Only you can take the wheel and chart a course. Where will you and your Process go?

As you continue your personal journey, I'd like to leave you with Dale Wimbrow's poem as additional guidance and inspiration.

THE GUY IN THE GLASS

by Dale Wimbrow, (c) 1934

When you get what you want in your struggle for pelf,
And the world makes you King for a day,
Then go to the mirror and look at yourself,
And see what that guy has to say.
For it isn't your Father, or Mother, or Wife,
Who judgement upon you must pass.
The feller whose verdict counts most in your life
Is the guy staring back from the glass.

He's the feller to please, never mind all the rest,
For he's with you clear up to the end,
And you've passed your most dangerous, difficult test
If the guy in the glass is your friend.

You may be like Jack Horner and "chisel" a plum,
And think you're a wonderful guy,
But the man in the glass says you're only a bum
If you can't look him straight in the eye.

You can fool the whole world down the pathway of years,
And get pats on the back as you pass,
But your final reward will be heartaches and tears
If you've cheated the guy in the glass.

ACKNOWLEDGMENTS

There are always so many people to thank (but never too many). I don't believe there is such a thing as a self-made man; for me, it's simple. If you know my name, and we have had a conversation, then I immediately thank you. No matter how long we spoke or whether we went back and forth through text or email, you had some impact on my life. You directly impacted my Process; at one point (or perhaps on more than one occasion), you were a part of The Process.

For those of you whose stories I shared, your personal struggles and victories helped me during my journey. You enabled me to see I was not alone, that failure and victory are mere moments, and so much more is still to come. Your Process was so incredibly valuable I wanted to share your story with the world. I could have written so much more about each of you; unfortunately, there's only so much room.

To all those I've served with throughout my career—sailors, soldiers, marines, airmen, and civilian personnel—it's been my pleasure and I commend you. You're doing something that less than one percent of the U.S. population has chosen to do. My fire to serve continues to burn bright because of you.

To my editors: Elizabeth, Diana, Leah, and April, all I can say is you turned my writing into something elegant, effective, and enlightening and I cannot thank you enough. To Sam, my strategist and branding master, and the entire Greenleaf team—*Exceptional Every Day* would still be only words in my journal, transcribed and saved on my desktop, without all of your efforts. Because of you, I believe any reader (or listener) can use my story to become better, day after day.

To Dr. Dawn Bragg: if it were not for you taking a chance on a non-traditional medical school applicant, this book would likely never have been written and my ability to influence and direct those experiencing some sort of struggle would never have been realized. And to Dr. Michael McBride—without your guidance during my time at the Medical College of Wisconsin, I would surely have lost sight of what really matters in caring for patients and helping them improve their lives.

Dr. Cindy Chang and Dr. Sara Edwards, I cannot thank your kindness in helping me land a fellowship spot with mere words. I am getting to do exactly what I have dreamt of doing ever since I was a child. I am realizing my Process.

To the crew at Southwest Sports Medicine and Orthopaedics and Baylor University, thank you for taking a chance on an active duty Navy physician. The environment and expertise you provided during my fellowship was second to none.

To those of you that I continue to cherish as my mentors—John Maxwell, Seth Godin, John Berardi, James Caylor, Dr. Ken Hagan, Dr. Mark Niedfeldt, Dr. Mark Greenawald, Dr. William Roberts, Dr. Wendy Arnold, Admiral Karl Thomas, Captain Tony Laird, Captain Brad "Brick" Conners, Drs. Dean and Dian Vieselmeyer, Dr. Ken Ebel, Dr. James Chung, and others who have come and gone through the years—my words will not do justice to your impact on me.

To Lydia, Tuesday, Julie, Jennifer, and Michael: thank you for being my biggest fans and showing me what true love really is. Sorry I had to leave.

Heather, you proved that there is always plenty of life left to be lived no matter what has already been accomplished. Your example, although crazy at times, is one so many can learn from as we chase our dreams and fulfill our desires.

To my great friends—Andrew, Todd, Adam, Mark, Chris, Caitlin, James, Jared, Greg, Trent, Brendan, Ryan, Emmanuel, and Jon—I would not be who I am if not for your love and kindness and the true belief you've had in me for so many years.

To Ed and Nora Hibsman: without you coming into my family's life, my girls would never have truly understood the value of family, love, and friendship.

The Travers allowed us to become their second family. The love you've shown us is beyond anything we could have ever imagined.

Carrole, Bill, and David, I owe you my life and love. You took me in as one of your family back in the small town of Fort Bragg; without you, I surely would not be here today to tell this story.

To my father and mother: if it were not for you, I would surely not be the person I am today. Our struggles have allowed me to make a difference in many lives.

Cousin Rich, you were the instrument that kept me yearning to surpass mediocrity. Thank you for teaching me so much.

To my wife, Danika, for putting up with everything involved in my Process and giving up parts of your life to help me figure out mine. I am forever indebted to you. This book is my way of telling you how grateful I am—if only I'd figured out how to include a lamb recipe or two or invested some of the publishing money into building a kitchen. You have truly sacrificed.

And finally, to Elle and Siena, my shining stars. My vision was to create something that I could pass on to you. From the beginning, I told the Greenleaf team I didn't care if one person bought the book as long as I established some sort of legacy, a way for The Process to continue, for my girls. Thank you for the love, tears, support, and all the laughs. May your Process be exactly what you want and make it to be.

And to everyone else in my life who has come and gone (and is perhaps still around), my thanks to you is no less valuable than anyone else. I wish you all the very best. Believe in The Process and the rest will fall in to place.

Gratias vobis ago. Muito obrigado. Thank you.

APPENDICES

APPENDIX A

YOUR DAILY TABLE

Fill out the graphic so it reflects who currently sits at your daily Table.

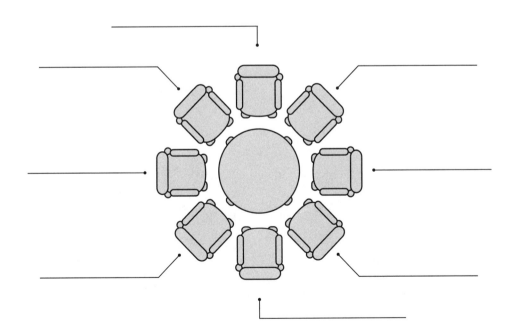

APPENDIX B

THE PROCESS CHECKLIST

In the space provided, or in your own journal, jot down a few ways you are going to make each of these items a priority in your life.

Priority 1—You

_____

_____

_____

Priority 2—Your Why

_____

_____

_____

Priority 3—Your One Thing

_____

_____

_____

Priority 4—Your Daily Table

_____

_____

_____

Priority 5—Your Work and Passion

_____

_____

_____

Priority 6—Your Family and Friends

_____

_____

_____

Priority 7—Your Mind and Body

_____

_____

_____

Priority 8—Spirituality and the Soul

_____

_____

_____

Priority 9—Rest, Play, and Sleep

_____

_____

_____

Priority 10—Something Bigger Than You

_____

_____

_____

APPENDIX C

YOUR PROCESS MAP

Fill out the Process Map to reflect your new priorities (your Process).

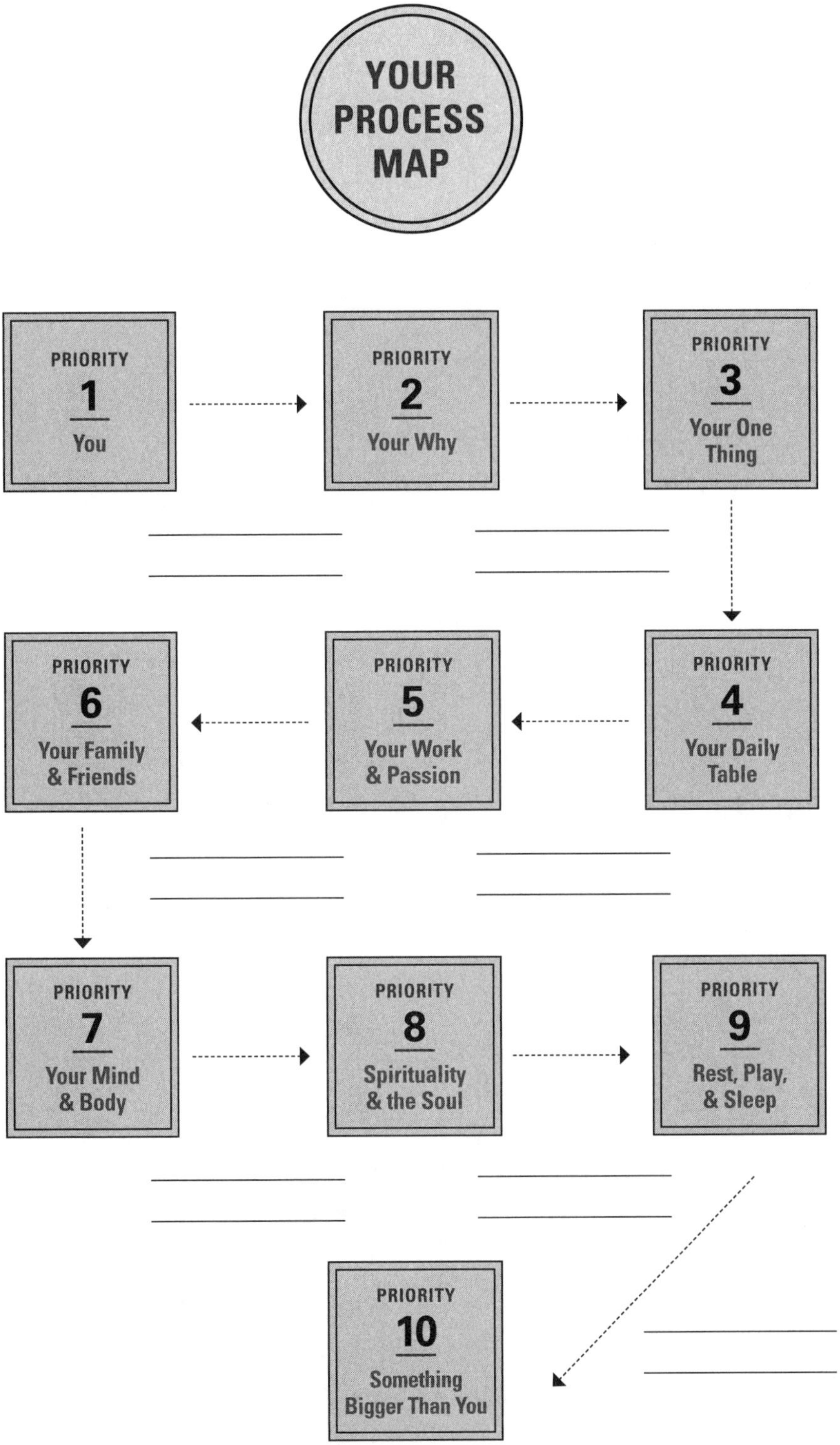
YOUR PROCESS MAP
PRIORITY 1 You
PRIORITY 2 Your Why
PRIORITY 3 Your One Thing
PRIORITY 4 Your Daily Table
PRIORITY 5 Your Work & Passion
PRIORITY 6 Your Family & Friends
PRIORITY 7 Your Mind & Body
PRIORITY 8 Spirituality & the Soul
PRIORITY 9 Rest, Play, & Sleep
PRIORITY 10 Something Bigger Than You

INDEX

D

E

M

N

O

P

T

U

V

W

resilience of, 30–31
self-awareness in, 14–15
Woods, Eldrick Tont (Tiger),
    154–55
work
    checklist, 78–79
    combining passion and, 74
    delaying gratification, 68–71
    lacking passion, 75–77
    living within means, 69–71
    money management, 71–72
    patience, 73–74
    taking care of basic necessities,
    67–68

Y

Your Mind and Body checklist,
    114–15
Your One Thing
    checklists, 52–53
    finding, 44–45
    keeping alive, 46–51
    mentors, 46–48

ABOUT THE AUTHOR

JASON VALADÃO is a husband, father to two amazing girls, friend and colleague to many, and a family and sports medicine physician, serving on active duty in the United States Navy. Before becoming a physician, he served as a naval flight officer during Operations Iraqi and Enduring Freedom. During his naval career, he taught in the Department of Naval Science at the University of California Berkeley, where he also spent three years as a faculty fellow and volunteer with the football team's coaching staff and earned a master's degree in education. Since 2009, he has served as an adjunct professor for Concordia University Irvine's master's degree program in coaching and athletic administration, and in 2017 he joined the faculty of the American Academy of Family Physicians Chief Resident Leadership Development Program helping to develop the physician leaders of tomorrow. His passion for leadership and personal growth led Jason to become a certified coach, speaker, and trainer with the John Maxwell Team, where he coaches people on their journeys toward personal growth and development.